SUPPER WITH
Charlie Bigham

FAVOURITE FOOD
FOR FAMILY & FRIENDS

PHOTOGRAPHY BY DAVID LOFTUS

MITCHELL BEAZLEY

For Claire –
who's been there every
step of the way and without
whom this book would
never have happened.

I've been lucky enough to work in the wonderful world of food for more than 25 years.

During that time, people have often suggested I should write a cookbook. So here it is – an eclectic mix of the dishes that my family and I cook and share with friends.

The food I like comes from many sources and I've always adapted recipes to my own tastes; I'm less interested in the definitive blueprint of a dish, but rather the version I find straightforward to cook and worth the effort. In this book, as well as my family classics, I've included a few recipes picked up over the years from the properly talented chefs I've worked with. And of course, throughout, you'll find a good smattering of my favourite recipes from the Charlie Bigham's kitchen – such as the fish pie, lasagne and chicken tikka masala – so, if you have a large number of people coming round, you can cook one dish to share.

My love of food started early. Childhood summers progressed from making mud pies and tearing around on bikes to messing about in boats as a teenager. Each day ended with my family sitting down and having supper together. This was the 1970s and ingredients were limited; supermarkets didn't even arrive near us until the late 1980s. We had to be inventive with the storecupboard and did a lot of foraging, whether that was mussels and cockles picked from the shore, or blackberries from the hedgerows. This was also when I started to learn how to cook. My mum taught me how to make my first lasagne and chocolate mousse (good staples of any 1970s dinner party) and I was soon putting together giant summer puddings or knocking up tasty smoked mackerel pâté. As you'll see in these pages, I still do.

In my student years, people tended to congregate at my flat because I was always happy to make supper for as many as turned up. The overall experience wasn't particularly gourmet: perhaps a very suspect mousse (which somehow contained eggs and canned beef consommé) or a tuna pasta salad with kidney beans, mayonnaise and sweetcorn – a proper student budget option. (Don't worry, I haven't included those here!) I suspect it was the copious quantities of £2.99 Bulgarian red wine that was both the bigger draw and made it all taste better.

Then it was on to the world of work for me, and the bright lights of London. The 1990s city was on lift-off in terms of the food scene. I lived just off the Portobello Road and my flatmate and I would head to the market late on Saturday afternoons to see what we could pick up for a song as it closed up. Among the specialist food shops was Mr Christian's deli, where I ended up working for a few months – piled high with unbelievable quantities of bread and pâtisserie; Birgit Erath's fantastic emporium of exotics that is The Spice Shop, and Garcia's, a visit to which is like a quick trip to Spain. Notting Hill was also a place where chefs were experimenting. There was Peter Gordon's Sugar Club, just around the corner from us on the All Saints Road; the eccentric L'Artiste Assoiffe (complete with parrots); Alistair Little's Ladbroke Grove outpost; or, when we were really pushing the boat out, the smarter bit of Notting Hill and Rowley Leigh's Kensington Place or Sally Clarke's. My favourite restaurant of all was The Mandola, a Sudanese place, for falafel and ful medames.

In short, living off Portobello Road in my twenties was food paradise and it was around this time that I really got stuck into cooking and

experimenting in the kitchen. For the first time, I made babaganoush, cooked with squid and monkfish, and tried slow-roasting lamb – all recipes you'll find in this book.

All good things come to an end. My days as a management consultant were definitely over and I needed to work out what to do with my life. What better place to do this than in a clapped-out VW campervan on a meandering journey to the Middle East and beyond? And so my girlfriend Claire and I set off on an adventure: we were after travel, culture and – of course – food.

For nine months, we drove through France, Italy and Greece, then into Turkey, Syria, Jordan, back into Turkey, on to Iran, over the border into Pakistan and – finally – to India. Along the way, we bought delicious food in markets to cook in the van or over a campfire. We also had some surprising meals at unlikely moments, such as an extraordinary feast in Istanbul with 14 courses of fish, eaten overlooking the Black Sea and ending with a whole sea bass encased in salt, broken open at the table with a mallet.

A couple of recipes inspired by that journey have made it into this book: the simple yet utterly delicious rabbit ragù pappardelle we ate in the hills above Venice and the Adana kebabs eaten in the city of that name, not far from the Syrian border. Our cooking equipment may have only been a two-ring burner in the van, supplemented by a small charcoal griddle for outdoor cooking, but we had some mighty meals. Special food doesn't need to be complicated.

After we returned, Claire and I got married; our own family life and kitchens were to come. As for work, I had always been entrepreneurial and liked making stuff: even just after leaving school, I sold the plates I made for my A-level in ceramics (and kept some, still in use today).

What I wanted was this: to do something I loved. With food, I had found that you learn something new every single day, and, if you're really interested, everything broadens and deepens your knowledge. So why not spend my working life in that world? Charlie Bigham's began at my kitchen table – packing all the ingredients into homemade paper bags – and once we had won orders from a handful of independent food shops, we moved to a small unit in north-west London. As we grew, we added our Quarry Kitchen in Somerset (see opposite).

My love of food is at the centre of everything, not least my business, and here it is, in the form of this cookbook: the favourite recipes that my family and I eat at home – our supper – and now yours, too!

Our big kitchen

When I started Charlie Bigham's, the problem I wanted to solve was this: any 'convenience food' usually came in packets with labels that read more like a chemistry lesson than a recipe (full of preservatives and nasties and a surprising amount of sugar) and didn't strike me as something I wanted to eat. Then, as now, I loved cooking, but on the odd busy day I'd want a day off from cooking from scratch. Wouldn't it be great to grab a bag of prepared ingredients and have a delicious fresh meal on the table in just ten minutes? It would save a lot of time, with no compromise on taste. That idea was the start:

food 'kits' – perhaps meat in a marinade and some chopped vegetables – that were ready to put in a pan. Next came pies in ceramic pots, then dishes that you put in the oven to finish off. For these, we found wooden containers that dramatically reduced the problem of plastic, and visually set us apart from other packaged food. We now have a 400-acre forest in south-west France growing poplar trees especially for us.

I started the company in London, and we still operate in the same area – Park Royal – an extraordinary district full of small food businesses, where some 20,000 people make food within a one-mile radius. The newer, eco-designed Quarry Kitchen in Somerset, named after the site that sits in a disused stoneworks, focuses on our bestsellers, such as lasagne. The high-ceilinged main room in Somerset is full of natural light and designed to be an inspiring place to work, as well as super-efficient. It has the same footprint as Wells Cathedral nearby, and I like to think of it as our temple to good food! Both kitchens are, of course, rather bigger than my kitchen at home, but not as different as you might think. They are kitchens, not factories, where we make food largely by hand, in small batches.

We are fussy about what goes into our dishes. Around 150 sorts of fresh ingredients are delivered every morning, and most of those are supplied by family-run businesses with whom we have worked for many years. Just as at my home, we keep just a handful of frozen ingredients, such as lime leaves for East Asian curries. When it comes to our storecupboard ingredients, we have had a simple mantra from day one: nothing goes into our food at work that I wouldn't be happy to have in my kitchen at home – that is a founding principle. At work, there are development kitchens that are the same as domestic kitchens, and we blind taste our big-kitchen products against dishes made in those development kitchens, to check they are as good as could be made at home. In other words, we aim for an artisan's approach on a reasonable scale.

Food businesses often start small. As they grow, some end up cutting corners and compromising on what made them special. And the bigger you get, the more tempting that becomes. Process takes over, and shelf life and cost become the drivers, rather than quality. To counter this, a small team of us get together every week to taste our recipes and ensure nothing creeps in to take us away from my original vision of zero compromise on quality and a focus on flavour.

For the equipment in our kitchens, we like to keep it simple and keep it real. Everything is cooked in a frying pan, a saucepan or an oven … they are just a bit bigger than those I have at home!

But the processes are essentially the same. As with all good meals, the difference is in the details. To take just one example: chopping parsley badly can quite easily turn it into something that tastes like grass. Our team wash the fresh leaves, dry them, chop them with a blade that is sharpened every day, then dry them again. It's exactly what you might do at home, if doing it well.

In my home kitchen, I tend to be a little slapdash: whenever I cook I can't resist experimenting, so my recipes vary a bit each time, not always for the best! Conversely, at the Charlie Bigham's big kitchens we are obsessive: measuring and weighing everything very carefully, constantly looking and tasting to check for consistency. That's always a challenge when you're dealing with food, as fresh ingredients are never quite the same two days in a row. Vegetables are grown in fields that change, the weather varies, the season shifts … but it all makes life more interesting.

We evolve our dishes over time and classics such as the fish pie have had various tweaks over the years. It's tempting to experiment, for example by adding prawns or scallops. But sometimes less is more and, because we are obsessed, I like to think we now produce as good a fish pie as you might make at home. Of course, there are always a few dishes that don't take off commercially, but they're still tasty. I'm a big fan of game as a delicious and sustainable form of meat, but have never managed to sell venison, rabbit or wild boar in our Charlie Bigham's products. All the more reason to include recipes for them in this book, I think, alongside the more familiar meats such as chicken and lamb.

We know from customer surveys that cooks buy our food to have a night off and want to enjoy what they are eating, rather than it being just about convenience. I hope this book is useful for cooks on the nights when we are all making supper, whether that's an everyday meal or for a special occasion.

My home kitchen

What's in it

My kitchen is at the heart of family life, not only as a place to sit and eat, but somewhere to make food that is approachable, fun, not too fussy and full of flavour.

This is the list-y bit. Brace yourselves …

What you routinely keep in your larder and fridge is at the centre of a good kitchen: they are the ingredients we all lean on as the basis of supper. My fridge is seldom without:
- Greek yogurt
- a chunk of Parmesan
- lemons and limes
- a piece of chorizo and bacon lardons
- butter …
… and a pot of cream.

Most of these keep for weeks rather than days and are always on hand.

My must-have storecupboard staples are:
- olive oil
- red wine and balsamic vinegars
- Dijon mustard
- capers (our wonderful dog is called Caper)
- runny honey
- 70 per cent dark chocolate for cooking
- a vanilla pod or two
- dried fruits and nuts
- Kikkoman soy sauce
- tomatoes: chopped, passata and purée
- and oodles of different pulses, rice, pasta and noodles.

Then there's my spice tray, which sits near my stove ready to enliven many dishes. Black peppercorns and Maldon sea salt flakes, of course, and a number of jars that are used so regularly their contents never get a chance to lose their pungency, among them ginger, cumin, turmeric, chilli flakes and smoked paprika. There are also a few more unusual items, such as sumac and the Moroccan and Middle Eastern spice mixes ras el hanout and za'atar.

I'm not a great fan of freezers. In mine you won't find much more than a bag of homemade breadcrumbs, frozen puff pastry, an old milk container filled with homemade chicken stock, maybe a bag of frozen berries and lots of ice.

From cupboard and fridge you can rustle up a quick and delicious supper at the drop of a hat. Pasta with a tomato sauce is lifted to a whole new level with the addition of some capers, a bit of chopped chorizo and a grating of fresh Parmesan. Vegetables are elevated if you simply roast them in the oven with a little garlic and rosemary and then finish off with a dollop of Greek yogurt, a sprinkling of za'atar and perhaps a drizzle of pomegranate molasses (which I usually have in, but wouldn't describe as a 'staple'). It's easy to make a substantial salad if you have some orzo pasta or Puy lentils to hand. An almost-instant pudding comes from dried Hunza apricots and a bag of pistachio nuts. You will find all those in these pages.

I won't give a long list of kit for the perfectly equipped kitchen because, in reality, you can cook with virtually nothing: we had just two

pans in our campervan for nine months, after all. When it comes to pans, choose quality over quantity: heavy-based is what you are after. Knives are equally simple – a big one and a smaller one – the best you can afford that feel comfortable in your hand, plus a cheap serrated veg-paring knife. In terms of more substantial kit, for me it's a Kitchen Aid for the heavy-duty work of cakes (whisking eggs and cream) and making my Adana kebabs, and a Magimix for quick slicing and chopping. And then there's the frivolous stuff that I could do without, but which makes kitchen life easier, or is just good fun: my lovely wooden-handled oyster shucker and clamp; a brilliant almost self-cleaning garlic press; a meat thermometer; a mouli-légumes for smooth soups and sauces, and a Microplane grater.

I'm not keen on microwaves and have never owned one. For me, heat is important to food, whether it comes from a flame or an oven. There is a moment of magic when you apply heat to food – almost alchemy. If you take cheese and put it under the grill, you don't just end up with hot cheese, but with a bubbling, oozing, caramelising, wonderful spectacle. Something extraordinary and multisensory happens: roasting meat or vegetables look and smell delicious, but, if you get close, they even sound delicious. This is very much part of the style of my Charlie Bigham's food.

How I like to cook
My kitchen is where we get together as a family and with friends. More often than not, there's some music playing, perhaps a drink in hand (maybe a lovely daiquiri, my favourite cocktail, to be found on page 34) and everyone pitching in and making something. And I love extending this spirit to whoever is around … so beware if you turn up as a guest, as I might suggest you make a pudding, or some mayonnaise! Claire and I don't mind what anyone cooks, it's about getting involved. There isn't a 'right way' in cooking. You might make something

five times and it will turn out five different ways; that's half the fun of it. Imperfection and variation are all part of learning something new.

You often hear about food and conviviality, a good word that conjures up merriment and generosity. But too often it's associated with eating rather than preparation and I think that's a shame. One person slaving away on their own before everyone else arrives is an opportunity missed. Making food together and chatting is one of the best bits of the evening. And, of course, you can get a bit peckish while you're doing it, so I like to have a few snacks to eat as we go: a simple little morsel of bruschetta perhaps, or a lovely gougère or two to help that drink go down even better. I hope you'll find some inspiration for these in my Standing-Up Starters & Drinks chapter.

The chapters in this book follow the typical style of eating in my home. Sitting-Down Starters could also work as light suppers (or lunches) with bread or potatoes and veg or a salad thrown in. Mains for Two, Four or Six are recipes that are generally easy to scale up or down, while Mains for Many contains dishes for times when you want to cook for a bigger party. Vegetable Sides & Sharing Plates is all about my style of food: a feast of lots of plates on the table for people to help themselves, which also works for flexitarian eating, as there will always be a choice. Puddings brings together a collection of my favourite classic sweet dishes, from the really simple to the more elaborate.

So let's get started. For the people who ask: 'What does Charlie cook at home?' This is it.

Standing-up starters & drinks

Classic tomato & basil bruschetta

What could be simpler than a few tomatoes on toast? Not a lot, but that doesn't mean you should overlook this as a delicious pre-dinner snack. The secret, of course, is the quality of the ingredients: lovely fresh tomatoes, a drizzle of that rather posh-looking bottle of olive oil that someone gave to you as a present and is too good to cook with, and a smattering of herbs, all on top-notch bread, freshly toasted.

Feeds 6

Preparation time: 10 minutes

4 very ripe large vine tomatoes, different colours if you like

1 large banana shallot, or ½ red onion, finely chopped

1 tablespoon extra virgin olive oil, plus more to serve

2 teaspoons balsamic vinegar (not too sweet)

leaves from ½ small bunch of basil (about 10g / ¼oz)

good loaf of bread, ideally sourdough or fresh baguette

1 large garlic clove

sea salt flakes and freshly ground black pepper

Chop up the tomatoes into a small dice; no need to remove the skins or seeds in my opinion. Mix in a large bowl with the shallot or onion, olive oil and balsamic vinegar. Tear the basil leaves into small pieces and add them to the mix along with plenty of salt and pepper. Set aside.

Slice the bread and toast on a preheated hot griddle pan or barbecue, or in a toaster. Once toasted, rub each slice with the garlic clove. Arrange on a serving platter.

Just before serving, spoon your chopped tomato mixture on to the toasts, drizzle with a little extra olive oil and enjoy! (Don't do this too far ahead as the bread will quickly turn soggy.)

Parmesan custards & smoked mackerel toasts

Rowley Leigh is a food hero of mine: a brilliant chef, a masterful writer on food and a lovely man. A few years ago, one of my sons, Rohan, ended up working for Rowley when he was running the restaurant at the newly opened Design Museum in Kensington. A keen cook already, Rohan morphed into being a fantastic chef as he learned from a master of British food. I have been the beneficiary of that tutelage ever since! This is one of Rowley's most popular recipes. It surprises people when you offer it to them, but it hits the spot every time. Rowley recommends it is served with anchovy toast, but I've opted for a slightly milder version on the same theme: smoked mackerel toast. My recipe for this is on page 52, but don't worry if you can't find any smoked mackerel, as there's a backup plan.

Feeds 4

Preparation time: 10 minutes

Cooking time: 25 minutes

For the custard

150ml (¼ pint) milk

150ml (¼ pint) double cream

60g (2¼oz) Parmesan, finely grated

2 large egg yolks

pinch of cayenne pepper

sea salt flakes and freshly ground white pepper, or black pepper if you don't have white

For the toast

4 generous blobs (about 2 tablespoons) smoked mackerel pâté (see page 52 for homemade, or see tip)

8 thin slices of basic white sliced bread, crusts removed

Pour the milk and cream into a saucepan and bring to the boil, stirring occasionally. Whisk in almost all the Parmesan (holding back about 10g /¼oz) until melted. Pour the mix into a jug and set aside to cool until no hotter than lukewarm.

Preheat the oven to 160°C/140°C fan (350°F), Gas Mark 3. Whisk the egg yolks into the cream mixture until thoroughly combined, then add a generous pinch of salt, a little white pepper and the cayenne.

Place 4 small ramekins or other small ovenproof dishes or cups in a small, deep baking tray or roasting tin. Fill the ramekins with your custard and pour just-boiled water into the baking tray or roasting tin around them until it reaches comfortably halfway up the ramekins. Cover the whole thing with foil and cook for about 20 minutes, or until the custards are just set.

Meanwhile, prepare your smoked mackerel toasts. Spread a generous blob of mackerel pâté (or anchovy-butter paste) on 4 slices of bread and then place another 4 slices of bread on top before squishing together. Toast the resulting sandwiches in a toaster, or on a hot griddle pan, then cut into thin soldiers, ready to dip into the Parmesan custard.

Preheat the grill to hot.

Remove the ramekins from their water bath, place on a baking tray and sprinkle evenly with the reserved Parmesan. Just before serving, put the Parmesan custard ramekins under the hot grill for about 2 minutes, or until the cheese melts and begins to brown.

Serve the custards with small spoons and the toasts for dipping.

Charlie's tip If you don't have any smoked mackerel pâté to hand, you can substitute a thin scraping of the anchovy paste Gentleman's Relish – an old-fashioned but rather wonderful spread – mixed to taste with 4 teaspoons whipped butter.

Gougères

A gougère is a special treat: effortlessly sophisticated and definitely a bit cheffy. These little mouthfuls of cheesiness are well worth making every now and again and are perfect if you've got a few people around for a drink or two, as well as for a standing-up starter. They are bound to impress, and you never need tell anyone how easy they are to make. In essence, a gougère is simply choux pastry (the same sort used for éclairs or profiteroles) flavoured with cheese. The secret is making sure the cheese you choose is top-notch. I've used the classic Gruyère in this recipe, but you can make mighty fine gougères with a good mature Cheddar, perhaps mixed with a little Parmesan.

Makes 25

Preparation time: 20 minutes

Cooking time: 20–25 minutes

100ml (3½fl oz) water

40g (1½oz) butter

60g (2¼oz) plain flour

2 eggs, lightly beaten

1½ teaspoons Dijon mustard

¼ teaspoon freshly ground nutmeg

¼ teaspoon paprika

¼ teaspoon fine sea salt

90g (3¼oz) Gruyère cheese, finely grated, plus 15g (½oz) for the tops

Put the water and butter into a large saucepan and place over a medium heat until the butter melts and the water comes to the boil. Immediately add the flour to the saucepan and stir well until a dough starts to form. Cook for 2 minutes, stirring constantly, but don't let it burn! Remove from the heat, tip into a large mixing bowl and leave to cool for 5 minutes.

Meanwhile, preheat the oven to 220°C/200°C fan (425°F), Gas Mark 7. Line a large baking tray, or 2 smaller trays, with nonstick baking paper or reusable baking liners.

Once the dough has cooled a little, start beating in the eggs using an electric hand whisk. Just add a little at a time, whisking well between each addition (you can also do this by hand). Once the dough is looking thick, smooth and glossy, whisk in the mustard, nutmeg, paprika and salt and then stir in the cheese until combined.

Transfer the mixture to a piping bag fitted with a large plain nozzle, if you have it; this can be a bit messy, but don't worry! Pipe the cheese mixture on to the prepared tray, aiming for around 25 small blobs each the size of a small walnut. You need to leave a good amount of space between each so they have room to expand as they cook. If you don't have a piping bag, you can put generous teaspoons of the mixture on the tray instead.

Sprinkle the extra cheese over the gougères. Bake for 15–20 minutes, or until puffed up and golden brown. They should be crisp on the outside and warm and just a little gooey on the inside.

Devils on horseback

Many moons ago, we made a range of Christmas canapés at Charlie Bigham's to ensure nobody went hungry at all those seasonal drinks parties. It was quite an operation: we made them all fresh every day, starting at the beginning of December all the way through to New Year's Eve. In our busiest year, we made more than five million canapés! This recipe is an old classic, but a classic done well, and I still knock up a few at home every Christmas.

Feeds 20 / Makes about 60

Preparation time: 20 minutes, plus overnight soaking

Cooking time: 10–12 minutes

500g (1lb 2oz) pitted Agen prunes, semi-dried rather than soft (you need 60 prunes)

3 Earl Grey teabags

250ml (9fl oz) water

100ml (3½fl oz) brandy

30 thin-cut streaky bacon rashers

Tip the prunes into a large mixing bowl, add the teabags, cold water and the brandy. Stir well, cover and leave to soak overnight.

Line 2 baking trays with baking paper or reusable baking liners. Lay out the bacon on a work surface and cut each rasher in half. Drain the prunes. Wrap each prune with a half-rasher of bacon and spear each with a cocktail stick. Place the wrapped prunes on the prepared baking trays. (You can prepare these several hours ahead and keep them in the fridge.)

When you are ready for your party, preheat the oven to 220°C/ 200°C fan (425°F), Gas Mark 7. Cook the devils for 10–12 minutes, or until the prunes are hot and the bacon crisp. Leave to cool for at least 5 minutes before serving.

White anchovies with parsley & garlic

There's no need to make food complicated and tasty appetisers don't come much simpler than this. High-quality anchovies are the most delicious fish, generally sustainable and exceptionally healthy, loaded with all that good omega-3 we need more of. Good brown anchovies can be found in a can, if you know what you're looking for. But I tend to go for the fresh white anchovies, sometimes called boquerones, usually sold in oil and vinegar or a light dressing. They are found at your local deli counter, or in the chilled section of good supermarkets. With this dish, a careful bit of shopping does most of the work for you!

Feeds 6–8

Preparation time: 5 minutes

about 300g (10½oz) white anchovies in oil, or lightly dressed

leaves from a large bunch of flat leaf parsley (about 50g / 1¾oz), finely chopped

3 garlic cloves, crushed

loaf of sourdough bread

½ lemon

extra virgin olive oil

Mix (thoroughly) the anchovies, parsley and garlic in a mixing bowl.

Slice and toast the sourdough bread, in a toaster or on a griddle pan.

Spoon the anchovies on to the slices of toasted sourdough.

Finely grate over a few strands of lemon zest, drizzle with olive oil, then serve.

Arancini

Whenever I cook risotto, I am careful to make more than I need, because the following day (or even a day or two later, if you chill the rice quickly) you can have some fun knocking up tasty little arancini balls. They are another of those almost-universally popular things to hand around with a drink.

Makes 20

Preparation time: 20 minutes

Cooking time: 20 minutes

60g (2¼oz) mozzarella cheese, preferably buffalo mozzarella, drained

400g (14oz) cold risotto (see opposite if making from scratch)

50g (1¾oz) Parmesan, finely grated, plus more to serve

25g (1oz) plain flour

2 large eggs, lightly beaten

100g (3½oz) dried white breadcrumbs

leaves from ½ bunch of flat leaf parsley (about 15g / ½oz), finely chopped

about 1 litre (1¾ pints) sunflower oil, to deep-fry

sea salt flakes and freshly ground black pepper

Cut or tear the mozzarella into small pieces each the size of a small hazelnut (2–3g / ⅛oz).

Mix the cold risotto with 40g (1½ oz) of the Parmesan. Take a generous dollop, about 25g (1 oz), and, with wetted hands – to prevent sticking – roll into a small ball about the size of a walnut. Make an indent in the ball and then squish in a piece of mozzarella before closing over. Set aside on a plate. Repeat until all your risotto is used up.

Prepare 3 shallow bowls, the first with the flour, the second with the eggs and the final dish with the breadcrumbs and parsley mixed together and seasoned with salt and pepper. Dip each ball in the flour, shake off the excess, then coat in the egg, and finally in the breadcrumbs. Set the breadcrumbed arancini balls on a plate.

Pour the sunflower oil into a large saucepan, at least 5cm (2 inches) deep, but no more than halfway up the sides of the pan. Set over a medium heat until the oil measures 180°C on a digital cooking thermometer, or, if you don't have a thermometer, until a cube of bread dropped into the oil browns in about 1 minute. Do not let the oil overheat and do not leave the pan unattended.

Using a slotted metal spoon, carefully lower the arancini balls into the hot oil one at a time, in batches of 4–5, keeping them apart. Each batch will take 3–4 minutes to cook. They are done when the coating has turned golden brown and crisp. Lift out with the slotted spoon on to a plate lined with kitchen paper to blot any excess oil.

Serve the arancini warm with a sprinkling of finely grated Parmesan over the top.

Charlie's tip Rather than mozzarella at the centre of your arancini, you can switch it for something else. I've found they're delicious with crab, or shredded ham hock.

Basic risotto

Makes enough for 20 arancini

Preparation time: 5 minutes

Cooking time: 25 minutes

1 large onion, finely chopped

50g (1¾oz) butter

250g (9oz) arborio rice

¼ bottle (about 200ml / 7fl oz) inexpensive white wine

750ml (1¼ pints) hot chicken stock, or vegetable stock

2 tablespoons double cream (optional)

To kick off your risotto, place a sauté pan or large saucepan over a medium heat. Cook the onion in the butter until nicely softened (5–10 minutes), stirring occasionally. Tip in the rice, crank up the heat to high and pour in the wine. Stir until all the wine has been absorbed.

Reduce the heat and add the stock a ladle at a time, stirring as you go (I keep my stock simmering on a low heat next to the risotto pan). Each time the stock is absorbed by the rice, add another ladleful. Continue until the rice tastes cooked, but still retains a modicum of bite right at the centre of the grains.

Right at the end, I stir in the slosh of cream for that extra bit of indulgence, but this is entirely optional.

Remove from the heat, leave to cool, then chill overnight.

Crab surprise

One of my favourite places to be in the summer is on a boat out on the sea. My summer holidays really start once I've put my lobster pot out; I've only got one. A couple of times over the summer, if we are lucky, we might catch a lobster, but more frequently we'll pull up the pot and find crabs. Our record catch is 42 crabs in one haul, all crammed into a standard-sized lobster pot and the majority a good size and perfect for eating: a day never to be forgotten. A more frequent catch is three or four, which are duly boiled up and dealt with using a hammer and crab pincers. Before you know it, someone has pinched all the white meat, perhaps for tasty crab sandwiches for lunch. The problem I am invariably left with is this: what to do with the brown meat? The answer was provided by talented chef Neil Nugent, who cut his teeth working in Michelin restaurants, though I got to know him when he was Executive Chef at Waitrose. I can't remember if Neil had a name for this rich and delicious dip when he gave me the recipe, but my family quickly christened it 'Crab Surprise', because it's both surprisingly good and usually appears as the surprising second crab dish of the day! Not only is this easy to make, it's also a fantastic way to ensure nothing goes to waste. If you are not starting with whole crabs, you can buy brown meat online; it's much less expensive than the white meat or claws.

Feeds 6–8

Preparation time: 10 minutes, plus at least 2 hours setting

Cooking time: 25 minutes

100g (3½oz) butter

1 large onion, finely sliced

2 garlic cloves, finely chopped

brown meat from 3 cooked crabs, or 300g (10½oz) ready-prepared brown crabmeat

400g (14oz) can of chopped tomatoes

generous squeeze of tomato purée

generous pinch of chilli flakes

a pinch of ground coriander

juice of 1 lemon

sea salt flakes and freshly ground black pepper

toast, to serve

Melt the butter in a frying pan, add the onion and cook over a low heat for 10 minutes, adding the garlic after 5 minutes and stirring occasionally until the onion is softened. Meanwhile, scrape the brown meat out the crab shells, if using.

Add the can of tomatoes to the onions with the tomato purée, chilli flakes, ground coriander and season generously with salt and pepper. Stir well and cook for a further 10 minutes, stirring every now and then, until the sauce has thickened. Add the crab and lemon juice and cook for a final 2–3 minutes, stirring.

Remove the pan from the heat, cool for a few minutes, then empty the entire contents into a food processor. (Or, if using a stick blender, you don't need to cool first.) Blend well for 1–2 minutes, or until you have a smooth sauce consistency. Decant the crab surprise into small bowls, ramekins or a larger serving dish and put in the fridge to set for around 2 hours. Serve with fingers of hot toast on the side.

Oysters au naturel

I love oysters. In fact, they are possibly my favourite food and would definitely feature in my Death Row meal! I think the best way to eat them is au naturel: fresh from the sea, prised open, nestled into a dish of crushed ice, then swiftly guzzled down with nothing more than a dash of lemon juice, some shallot dressing and a spot of Tabasco. My advice is to make sure you give the oyster a good chew before you swallow it (some people advise swallowing without chewing, which is very perplexing as you then deny yourself most of that wonderful sea flavour and swap it for a rather unattractive swallow). Over the years I've converted a good few oyster virgins to the pleasures of this ultimate shellfish experience, though some people need a helping hand with the idea of them being raw. For these slightly more timorous souls, I recommend a cooked oyster – a simple recipe for these is overleaf.

Feeds 6

Preparation time: about 20 minutes, depending on your shucking skills

2 dozen fresh, live oysters

crushed ice

2 lemons, cut into wedges

small bottle of Tabasco sauce

For the dressing

1 large banana shallot, or 3 small shallots, very finely chopped

3½ tablespoons red wine vinegar

1–2 teaspoons Dijon mustard

Shuck the oysters (see tip, below), then loosen the oysters from the shells. Place the oyster in its rounded half-shell on a bed of crushed ice. Arrange lemon wedges among the oysters.

For the dressing, the finer you chop the shallot, the better. Put the chopped shallot in a small dish, then add the red wine vinegar and the Dijon mustard, to taste. Stir together.

As you eat the oysters, put a dab of the shallot dressing, a squeeze of lemon juice and a drop of Tabasco into each. Chew, close your eyes, taste the sea, then swallow.

Charlie's tip Oysters will keep in the fridge for about four days. Only use those that are undamaged and firmly closed, or close when tapped on a work surface. Once you've got the knack, shucking oysters is a satisfying pastime and a sure way to impress your family and friends. Invest in a proper oyster shucker (basically, a short stubby knife) and ideally, if you can find one, also an oyster clamp to hold the oyster. If you don't have an oyster clamp, I suggest you use a tea towel folded over several times. This grips the oyster and means, if the knife slips, you will not stab your hand.

Put the oyster on a work surface (or in your clamp) flattest-side up and use your probing shucker to find the place to insert the blade into the pointed hinge-end of the shell. Twist to release the hinge, then move your knife laterally along the top side of the shell until you cut through the oyster's muscle; the shell will then open easily. Remove the top shell. Holding the oyster carefully, so you do not lose the tasty juices, use your knife to carefully cut free the oyster meat from the muscle holding it to the rounded half of the shell. Put the oysters on a serving tray as you go. Take a look at www.charliebighams.com/cookbook to see me have a go.

Oysters with a saffron velouté

A dish that is useful when cooking for the oyster novice – who might find cooked oysters less challenging than raw – and also a good showy recipe for a bit of fun and indulgence.

Feeds 6

Preparation time: 30 minutes

Cooking time: 15 minutes

---

2 dozen fresh, live oysters

small jar of lumpfish caviar (optional)

small bunch of dill (about 20g / ¾oz, optional)

For the sauce

25g (1oz) butter

1 large banana shallot, or 2 smaller shallots, finely chopped

1 garlic clove, finely chopped

3½ tablespoons white wine

good pinch of saffron threads

4 teaspoons plain flour

300ml (½ pint) hot fish stock, fresh, or made with ½ fish stock cube

100ml (3½fl oz) double cream

freshly ground black pepper

First, make the sauce. Melt the butter in a saucepan over a medium-low heat and add the shallot and garlic. Fry gently for 3 minutes, or until softened, stirring regularly. Add the wine and saffron and simmer for 1–2 minutes, or until the liquid is well reduced, stirring occasionally.

Sprinkle the flour into the pan and stir it into the shallot mixture. Slowly add the stock, stirring well between each addition. Bring to a simmer and cook for 5 minutes, until the sauce is thickened and glossy, stirring constantly.

Reduce the heat to low and add the double cream and a couple of twists of black pepper; you shouldn't need any salt as the oysters will be naturally briny. Cook for a further 2 minutes, stirring. Take off the heat and blitz with a stick blender until smooth and a little frothy.

Preheat the oven to 220°C/200°C fan (425°F), Gas Mark 7.

Shuck the oysters (see tip on page 30), loosen them from their rounded half-shells and put on a baking tray. Cook for just 3 minutes. Remove from the oven, remove the oysters and stir the oyster liquid from the shells into the sauce. Quickly replace an oyster into each rounded half-shell and gently warm the sauce, if it's gone a little cold.

Spoon 1 tablespoon of warm saffron velouté over each oyster. Then, if you are feeling indulgent, top off each oyster with a small teaspoon of lumpfish caviar and a dill sprig. Serve with small spoons.

Daiquiri

A lot of the cooking I do is a communal affair, with family and friends in the kitchen chatting, everyone cooking a dish or otherwise helping out. It's usually not long before someone (probably me) suggests a drink might be nice, and this is the perfect moment for a cocktail. My first choice is the classic daiquiri. Made famous (but not invented by) Ernest Hemingway, it is elegant and delicious in its simplicity: rum, sugar and lime juice. You may be wondering: what about a strawberry daiquiri, or maybe a banana daiquiri? I was put right on this many years ago, when I wandered into a very smart, but very good, bar and asked the barman what daiquiris he had. He looked down his nose at me and told me there was only one daiquiri which he would make for me. He was correct: there is only one daiquiri. Here it is.

Makes 1

Preparation time: 3 minutes

50ml (1¾fl oz) white rum

25ml (1fl oz) freshly squeezed lime juice (about 1 juicy large lime), plus a slice of lime, to garnish

10ml (2 teaspoons) sugar syrup (see tip)

ice cubes and crushed ice

Put the rum, lime juice and sugar syrup in a cocktail shaker.
Add a couple of ice cubes and give a good shake for 10–12 seconds.

Put a generous amount of crushed ice into a martini glass.
Strain the cocktail into the glass and garnish with a lime slice.

Charlie's tip To make your own sugar syrup, stir together an equal amount of white sugar and water in a small saucepan and heat until dissolved. Leave to cool. You can make more than you need and keep it indefinitely in the fridge.

Cosmopolitan

I always think of a Cosmo as a party drink: it's great to kick off proceedings and somehow announces to everyone that you're in for a good evening. A properly made Cosmo is the perfect shade of pink, so they look great too. I even have a special pink tray (made by zazoodesign.com) that I reserve almost exclusively for loading up with them before handing them around. Although it is perhaps sacrilege to suggest this, I think it's fine to make a decent batch of the base cocktail mix a few hours in advance and then shake in the cranberry juice as your guests arrive.

Makes 1

Preparation time: 5 minutes

25ml (1fl oz) vodka

25ml (1fl oz) Cointreau, or Triple Sec liqueur

25ml (1fl oz) freshly squeezed lime juice (about 1 large, juicy lime)

10ml (2 teaspoons) sugar syrup (see page 34 for homemade)

50ml (1¾fl oz) cranberry juice

ice cubes

1 orange, for garnish

Put all your liquid ingredients in a cocktail shaker and fill it to the brim with ice cubes. Shake hard for 8–10 seconds, then strain into a martini or coupe glass.

Cut a piece of orange zest from your orange (I use a vegetable peeler), wipe it around the rim of the glass, then squish it over the drink to release the oil and float it on top.

White lady

To include cocktails in the book but exclude gin didn't feel right. Obviously, the classic gin cocktail is the Martini … but that seemed too obvious. Then I pondered the Tom Collins (well worth checking out: a nice summer option), but I've plumped for the lesser-known and very elegant White Lady (also known as a Delilah or Chelsea Side Car, take your pick). It packs a punch and is rather delicious. My recommendation is to stick to one only, though you are likely to be tempted to have a second …

Makes 1

Preparation time: 5 minutes

50ml (1¾fl oz) gin

20ml (¾fl oz) Cointreau, or Triple Sec liqueur

20ml (¾fl oz) freshly squeezed lemon juice

10ml (2 teaspoons) sugar syrup (see page 34 for homemade)

1 egg white

ice cubes

1 lemon, for garnish

Put all the liquid ingredients, including the egg white, into a cocktail shaker. Shake with no ice for 15 seconds (this is known as the dry shake).

Fill the shaker with ice cubes and shake for a further 15 seconds (this is the wet shake). Strain into a martini or coupe glass.

Cut a generous piece of zest from your lemon (I use a vegetable peeler), twist into a spiral and float it on top to garnish.

Espresso martini

If the Cosmopolitan is the party drink to start the evening, then the Espresso Martini is great to reserve for a little later on. Only invented in the 1980s, the story goes that it was the solution to a request from a supermodel when she asked for a drink, 'That will wake me up, then mess me up.' I would, obviously, urge restraint and settle for just the one drink, so you can be woken but spared the second part. When I have a party, I tend to knock up a few of these at midnight as a little adrenaline shot that keeps everyone going for another hour or two. I even have a sign at home, beautifully made by my daughter Petra, announcing the 'Midnight Espresso Martini Bar'. I've found that date syrup works really well, adding a rich depth (you can get it in health food shops or online). If you don't have any, just use the more traditional sugar syrup.

Makes 1

Preparation time: 5 minutes

35ml (1¼fl oz) vodka

15ml (½fl oz / 1 tablespoon) Kahlua

25ml (1fl oz) freshly made espresso

10ml (2 teaspoons) date syrup, or sugar syrup (see page 34 for homemade)

ice cubes

espresso coffee beans, to garnish (optional)

Pour all the liquid ingredients into a cocktail shaker and fill it right to the brim with ice cubes. Shake vigorously for 15 seconds, then strain into a coupe glass.

Top each drink with an espresso coffee bean if you like, then serve.

Sitting-down starters

Butternut squash soup with chilli & pine nuts

If you are anything like me, every now and again your eyes take a wander around the kitchen and fall, guiltily, on a couple of butternut squash (or celeriac, parsnips, or sweet potatoes) that have been sitting around for a little longer than they should have been. When this moment coincides with a pot of chicken stock – as it often does, in my kitchen – it's time to turn them into soup. I quite often knock up a pan of soup as a good way of filling the gaps when another dish is in the oven or bubbling away on the stove. It puts something in the fridge for tomorrow, but of course the main reason for making your own soup is that it just tastes better than anything you can lay your hands on that comes in a packet, tub or can.

Feeds 8

Preparation time: 15 minutes

Cooking time: 25–30 minutes

50g (1¾oz) butter

2 tablespoons olive oil

2 large onions, sliced

2 garlic cloves, sliced

2 butternut squashes, each about 1kg (2lb 4oz)

generous pinch of chilli flakes

saucepan of chicken stock (say around 1.5 litres / 2½ pints), or shop-bought (see tip)

100ml (3½fl oz) white wine

4 tablespoons pine nuts

200ml (7fl oz) double cream

handful of flat leaf parsley leaves, chopped

sea salt flakes and freshly ground black pepper

bread, to serve

Melt the butter in a large, heavy-based saucepan or casserole with the olive oil over a medium-low heat. Add the onions and garlic and cook for 5–6 minutes, or until the onions soften and just start to brown, stirring regularly.

Peel the butternut squashes with a veg peeler, cut in half, deseed, then cut into 2–3cm (1 inch) chunks. Add the butternut squash and chilli to the onion pan and give everything a good stir. Continue cooking for about 5 minutes, stirring every now and again to check nothing burns.

Once the squash has softened a little, add the stock and wine to the pan and bring to the boil. Reduce the heat slightly, cover loosely with a lid and simmer for 15–20 minutes, or until the squash is soft.

Meanwhile, toast your pine nuts in a small frying pan over a medium heat, stirring often and keeping a careful eye on them to ensure you don't burn them, as I often manage to! Set aside. (You can also toast the pine nuts for a few minutes in the oven, if it's on, again taking care not to burn them.)

Remove the squash from the heat, add 150ml (¼ pint) of the cream and blitz with a stick blender until you have a lovely velvety-smooth texture. Add salt and pepper, to taste. Return to the heat and warm through gently, stirring. To serve, ladle the soup into bowls and then finish with a swirl of the remaining cream, some chopped parsley and a sprinkling of toasted pine nuts. Serve with bread.

Charlie's tips

- If you don't have a pan of chicken stock on the go, shop-bought fresh stock is quite strong, so I suggest you use two 500ml (18fl oz) pouches or pots with 500ml (18fl oz) of water, or make up the 1.5 litres (2½ pints) of chicken stock with three cubes.
- If you want a finishing flourish for your soup, try a few drops of olive oil and balsamic vinegar.

Quick babaganoush with toasted pitta

I've made this recipe more than a hundred times and I don't think I've yet found someone who doesn't love it. I am not a babaganoush purist and apologise in advance to those who are. This recipe is great made the 'proper' way with slow burning of the aubergine skins over a beautiful charcoal fire, followed by careful scraping out of the flesh. I even – very occasionally – do that myself. But this is a quick recipe for people who might be in a bit of hurry but still want an easy, popular and delicious starter.

Feeds 6

Preparation time: 10 minutes, plus at least 1 hour chilling

Cooking time: 30 minutes

3 large aubergines

200ml (7fl oz) extra virgin olive oil, plus more to serve

1–2 garlic cloves, roughly chopped

juice of 1 large lemon

150g (5½oz) tahini

100ml (3½fl oz) water

sea salt flakes and freshly ground black pepper

To serve

paprika, smoked paprika, or sumac

toasted pitta

Preheat the oven to 220°C/200°C fan (425°F), Gas Mark 7. Trim the ends off the aubergines, then slice lengthways: each will produce about 5 slices. Lay out the slices in a single layer in a large, deep roasting tin, or 2 smaller tins, and sprinkle liberally with 150ml (¼ pint) of the olive oil.

Cook the aubergines for about 30 minutes, turning halfway, until softened and lightly browned in places.

In the meantime, put the garlic in a food processor or blender along with the lemon juice and remaining olive oil. Give it a good whizz until the garlic is well chopped up. Add the tahini and give it another whizz, gradually adding the measured water as you blend. Don't worry if your mixture splits at this point.

Next add the now-cooked aubergines and blend thoroughly (around 5 minutes). You are aiming for a smooth consistency, similar to thick yogurt. Add a generous amount of salt and pepper, to taste.

Decant the blended mixture into a serving dish, drizzling with a little olive oil and dusting with paprika, smoked paprika or sumac. Refrigerate (to set) for at least 1 hour, then serve with toasted pitta.

Three cheese soufflé

There are a few recipes that might seem a bit retro but stand the test of time. The cheese soufflé, a staple of the 1970s dinner party, is surely among them. I've never understood why people think soufflé is difficult to make. As long as you can make a white sauce, it couldn't be simpler and the chances of it not rising are zero (at least in my experience). The secrets are to make small soufflés in individual ramekins, rather than a large dish, make sure your oven is nice and hot when you put the soufflés in, then resist the temptation to have a peek to see how they are doing halfway through. Fans of Charlie Bigham's food might well find themselves with some ceramic pots in their cupboard from eating our pies. These make a pretty good soufflé dish, not least because they are larger than a standard ramekin, so you will end up with extra-large soufflés, if fewer of them!

Feeds 6

Preparation time: 15 minutes

Cooking time: 25 minutes

75g (2¾oz) butter, plus more for the ramekins

6 large eggs

75g (2¾oz) plain flour

450ml (16fl oz) milk

1 teaspoon Dijon mustard

50g (1¾oz) mature Cheddar, grated

50g (1¾oz) Comté cheese, grated

50g (1¾oz) Parmesan, finely grated

½ bunch of chives (about 15g / ½oz), finely chopped, plus more to serve

First, preheat the oven to 220°C/200°C fan (425°F), Gas Mark 7. Place a sturdy baking tray on the middle shelf of the oven to preheat. Take 6 ramekins (each about 250ml / 9fl oz in volume) and butter the insides generously.

Separate the eggs. Put the whites into a large mixing bowl. Whisk the yolks together in a smaller bowl and set aside.

Make a simple roux by melting the butter in a saucepan, mixing in the flour thoroughly with a wooden spoon and then slowly adding the milk, stirring well after each addition to ensure there are no lumps.

Add the mustard and all the three cheeses and continue to stir over a low heat until all the cheese is melted and you have a very thick sauce. Take the pan off the heat, beat in the egg yolks, then stir in the chives.

Whisk your egg whites with an electric hand whisk until they have formed peaks that are stiff but not dry. Using a large metal spoon, fold roughly one-fifth of the egg whites lightly into the cheese sauce. Then tip the cheese sauce into the mixing bowl and fold into the rest of the egg whites until you have an even consistency.

Spoon your soufflé mix into each prepared ramekin, filling to the top. Place all the ramekins on the preheated sturdy baking tray. Cook for 12 minutes, or until well risen and lightly browned. Serve immediately, sprinkled with chives.

Charlie's tip If you have some Stilton left over from Christmas, like I often do, you can use it up in these soufflés. I've found they might not rise quite as well, but are still very tasty.

Beetroot, red onion & blue cheese filo tart

I'm not sure why, but, for some reason, I thought I didn't like beetroot – it could have been a scarring childhood experience, or maybe it was that bright pink colour, which I now love. Then there came a day at work when one of our lovely chefs, Madalene, introduced me to the joys of beetroot. Matching the earthiness of beetroot to the sweetness of caramelised onions and blue cheese works well. And putting the whole lot in some crispy filo pastry works even better. Perfect for vegetarian guests, or just for veggie moments, they make a great starter.

Feeds 6

Preparation time: 20 minutes

Cooking time: 35–45 minutes

450g (1lb) raw beetroot, peeled and cut into 1cm (½ inch) chunks

olive oil

60g (2¼oz) butter, plus 25g (1oz) for the onions

3 red onions, finely sliced

270g (9¾oz) packet of filo pastry, defrosted if frozen (you may not need it all)

150g (5½oz) mild blue cheese, such as Dolcelatte or Saint Agur (I like my local, Dorset Blue Vinny)

6 thyme sprigs

sea salt flakes and freshly ground black pepper

Preheat the oven to 220°C/200°C fan (425°F), Gas Mark 7. Tip your prepared beetroot into a roasting tin, splash with olive oil, season with pepper and a small amount of salt, then bake for 25–30 minutes, or until tender. Reduce the oven temperature to 200°C/180°C fan (400°F), Gas Mark 6.

Meanwhile, melt the 25g (1oz) butter and 1 tablespoon olive oil in a frying pan and soften your sliced red onions with a pinch of salt over a medium heat for about 15 minutes, stirring occasionally, until soft and starting to brown.

As the onions cook, melt the 60g (2¼oz) butter in a small saucepan. Select 6 small metal tart cases (9–11cm / 3½– 4 inches in diameter) or a 12-hole muffin tin and generously brush with butter (you will serve 2 tarts per person if using the muffin tin).

Lay out your filo pastry flat on a large work surface. Brush the first layer of filo with butter, cut it into squares that fit into your tart cases or muffin moulds and layer them up, at a slight angle to each other, to form filo cases. You will need 3 layers of pastry in each. Repeat, buttering more sheets of filo, until you have the right number of buttered layers in each tart case or muffin mould.

Spread a layer of caramelised onion into each filo case, then a layer of roasted beetroot, and finally dollops or crumblings of blue cheese. Finish your tarts with thyme sprigs and a good grind of pepper. Cook in the oven for 10 minutes, or until the filo is golden brown. Serve with salad leaves, or on their own.

Courgette flowers with goats' cheese

If you grow courgettes, you can pick them young with the flowers and cook them like this, or keep an eye out for them in greengrocers and online. You might think this dish sounds a bit fiddly, but it's really not that tricky. Give it a go! The quantity of filling needed will depend on the size of your flowers; any left over is great spread on toast.

Feeds 4

Preparation time: 30 minutes

Cooking time: 10 minutes

400g (14oz) light, soft goats' cheese

finely grated zest of 1 lemon

12 large basil leaves, rolled up and cut into fine shreds, plus more to serve

pinch of chilli flakes

50g (1¾oz) plain flour, to dust

8–12 baby courgettes, with flowers attached (stamens removed)

1 litre (1¾ pints) sunflower oil, to deep-fry

sea salt flakes and freshly ground black pepper

For the batter

60g (2¼oz) self-raising flour

140g (5oz) cornflour, plus more if needed

1 teaspoon sea salt flakes

300ml (½ pint) fizzy water, plus up to 100ml (3½fl oz) more, if needed

To serve

2 tablespoons runny honey

60g (2¼oz) toasted pine nuts, crushed

Mix together the goats' cheese, lemon zest, shredded basil and chilli flakes in a bowl. Sprinkle the plain flour over a shallow dish and season it with salt and pepper. Line a baking tray with kitchen paper.

To stuff the flowers, transfer the goats' cheese mixture to a large piping bag fitted with a plain nozzle (or use a couple of teaspoons if you don't have one; it's a little messier but works fine). Unfurl the top of a flower, being careful not to tear it, and pipe or spoon a generous quantity of the mixture inside, then twist the top of the flower closed. Lightly roll the flower in the seasoned flour and set aside. Repeat with the other flowers: filling and flouring.

To make the batter, sift the flours with the salt into a large mixing bowl. Gradually add the fizzy water, mixing briefly with a large metal whisk until you have a light, smooth batter the consistency of single cream, adding more flour or water if necessary.

Pour the oil into a wok or large saucepan, at least 5cm (2 inches) deep. Set over a medium heat until the oil reaches 180°C (350°F) on a cooking thermometer or, if you don't have one, until a small piece of bread dropped into the oil browns in about 1 minute. Do not let the oil overheat and do not leave the pan unattended.

Pick up a courgette using metal tongs, dip it and the attached stuffed flower head into the batter until evenly coated all over, then shake to remove the excess batter. Very carefully, lower it gently into the hot oil and fry for about 1 minute, or until the batter is crisp and very golden brown. Using a slotted spoon, lift out on to the prepared tray lined with kitchen paper, to blot any excess oil.

Cook the others in the same way, in batches, 2–3 at a time, adding extra water to the batter if it thickens too much. Keep an eye on the temperature of the oil and turn the courgettes every now and then so they cook evenly.

Serve 2–3 courgettes with flowers on each plate, drizzled with honey and sprinkled with toasted pine nuts.

Halloumi saganaki

I love Greece, especially in early or late summer: clear blue skies, bright sunshine, azure waters and lovely, warm people. I always think that Greek cooking is a bit like English cooking, in that you can find delicious food, but you need to seek it out. Whenever I find myself in a Greek taverna, I'll scan the menu for this dish and invariably order it. It's a simple way to cook halloumi that elevates it to something even better. This is good served with salad leaves, or as part of a spread, when you have vegetarians at the table.

Feeds 4

Preparation time: 5 minutes

Cooking time: 5 minutes

2 x 250g (9oz) packets of halloumi cheese, drained

6 tablespoons fine semolina

3–4 tablespoons olive oil

4 tablespoons runny honey

2 teaspoons black sesame seeds

2 teaspoons white sesame seeds

leaves from a few oregano sprigs, or a sprinkle of dried oregano, if you don't have fresh to hand

freshly ground black pepper

Place the halloumi on a board and slice laterally through the middle of each block, to make them half their original thickness. You should end up with 4 rectangles of halloumi.

Sprinkle the semolina into a shallow bowl and dip the halloumi on both sides to coat. Set aside.

Pour 3 tablespoons of the oil into a large frying pan and place over a medium heat. Once hot, add the coated halloumi and cook for 2–3 minutes on each side until golden brown and crisp. Add a little extra oil if needed. Meanwhile, warm the honey in a small saucepan over a low heat, stirring.

Arrange the cooked halloumi on a serving dish, pour over the hot honey, then scatter with the sesame seeds and chopped or dried oregano. Finish off with a twist or so of black pepper.

The best smoked mackerel pâté

It is very possible that this is the best recipe in the book, so if you find yourself reading this on that desert island and have to hurriedly tear out just a single page before it is washed away by the waves, consider making it this one. My smoked mackerel pâté is a firm family favourite (and beyond), so much so that we had a small family debate on whether I was allowed to spill its secrets here. The debate was inconclusive … so here it is! Warning: it's so good that it's almost addictive. Once we had a young American staying with us for a couple of weeks and he couldn't stop himself eating it every day, for breakfast, lunch and supper. My quantities here are generous, but any leftovers don't last long.

There are two key things you need to make this pâté work. First off, you must have fresh mackerel (the adage that you should never let the sun go down on a mackerel is a good one). If you find yourself within striking distance of the British coast any time in the later summer months, you might well come across some freshly caught mackerel; if not, look out for them in your local fishmonger or buy them online (OK, they will arrive a day old but that's just about all right). The second thing you need is a hot-smoker. You can make one (even out of an old biscuit tin; look online for tutorials) but I'd recommend buying one – a basic type is fine.

Feeds 10

Preparation time: 20 minutes, plus at least 45 minutes chilling

Cooking time: 20 minutes

---

6 super-fresh mackerel, headed and gutted (alternatively, see tip)

150g (5½oz) butter

50g (1¾oz) horseradish sauce (I recommend Tracklements)

juice of 1 lemon

1 bay leaf for a single big dish, or small leaves if using ramekins

5 slices of white bread, for Melba toast, or decent sourdough or other bread, toasted

sea salt flakes and freshly ground black pepper

Hot-smoke the mackerel, using about 100g (3½oz) smoking sawdust. Either follow the manufacturer's instructions, or watch my lesson at www.charliebighams.com/cookbook. They will take about 20 minutes to cook. The mackerel will have taken on an orangey-brown hue and the cooked fish will easily come away from the bones.

Pick the flesh off the cooked fish, discarding any skin and bones. This is a delicate operation that takes a little practice and patience, but is worth doing properly, as bones will not improve your pâté.

Melt the butter in a small saucepan. Put the smoked mackerel, three-quarters of the melted butter, the horseradish and the lemon juice in a food processor and blend to a smooth paste. Season with salt and pepper, to taste.

Decant the pâté into a serving dish (or I often use individual ramekins), smooth down with a fork, then cover with a thin layer of the remaining melted butter. Finish with a bay leaf pressed gently into the butter. Refrigerate for at least 45 minutes before serving.

As this takes me back to my childhood, my favourite accompaniment to smoked mackerel pâté is that staple of the 1970s dinner party: Melba toast. Split the sliced white toasts in half through the middle, to make each into 2 super-thin slices, then place under a hot grill for 1 minute, or into a hot oven, until they become both crispy and curly. Otherwise, serve with normal toast.

Charlie's tip The magic of this recipe is significantly to do with the mackerel being freshly smoked. However, I have experimented with shop-bought smoked mackerel and, though it's a few notches down in taste, you can just about get away with it. The key is to buy hot-smoked mackerel (but not the overly orange stuff coated with black pepper). It is important you remove the skins from the mackerel before adding it to the pâté. The shop-bought mackerel will be drier than freshly home-smoked, so you need to compensate by adding some cream cheese. I use 200g (7oz) Philadelphia to 630g (1lb 6oz) hot-smoked mackerel. You will also need to be generous with your blending time, as you are aiming for a very smooth-textured pâté; expect it to take around five minutes.

Elderflower-cured salmon

A simple, quick dish that sings with summer freshness and takes mere minutes to make. When it comes to curing fish, the secret is to balance acidity with sweetness, so it's worth paying attention to the quantities in this recipe. I love the zing you get from freshly squeezed lime juice, while the elderflower adds great floral notes as well as sweetness. Serve with blinis – either homemade (delicious) or shop-bought – and crème fraîche.

Feeds 10

Preparation time: 15 minutes

500g (1lb 2oz) very fresh salmon fillet, skinned (in a single piece if possible, which makes things easier; see tip)

75ml (2¾fl oz / 5 tablespoons) lime juice (3–4 limes), plus the finely grated zest of 2 limes

25ml (about 2 tablespoons) elderflower cordial (I always have a bottle of excellent Belvoir cordial on the go)

50ml (3½ tablespoons) extra virgin olive oil

50g (1¾oz) baby capers, drained

1 fresh red chilli, finely sliced, or ½–1 teaspoon chilli flakes

sea salt flakes and freshly ground black pepper

Slice the salmon finely and then cut into pieces about 5cm (2 inches) long. Arrange on a flat, non-metallic dish. Pour over the lime juice, elderflower cordial and olive oil, ensuring all the salmon has some liquid on it.

Once you have applied this liquid the salmon will take around 10 minutes to cure (or 'cook'). It will change from the raw salmon translucence to a slightly milkier opacity when ready.

Finally, scatter over the capers, chilli or chilli flakes and lime zest and finish off with a sprinkling of salt and a twist or so of pepper. Serve immediately.

Charlie's tip To skin the salmon, place the fillet skin-side down on a work surface and use a sharp knife to cut down to the skin (start at the thinner end if you have a tail piece). Grip the end of the skin with your other hand and slide the knife along the skin under the flesh away from you, with the blade slightly angled towards the work surface, gently pulling the skin towards you at the same time.

Scallops with peas & chorizo

Scallops seem to have a near-universal appeal: not too fishy in flavour and with a lovely sweetness. They are a great introduction to eating and cooking shellfish. If they're not available at your fishmonger or the fish counter in a supermarket, you can always buy them online. And though fresh is best, there are also good-quality frozen scallops. This is my version of a classic of the chef Rowley Leigh, a simple dish of complementary flavours that looks great on the plate. My quantity is for a starter, but you can easily double up the recipe to make a great main course.

Feeds 6

Preparation time: 10 minutes

Cooking time: 10 minutes

---

18 good-sized scallops (3 each; for a main course I'd allow 5 or 6)

125g (4½oz) chorizo, ideally picante (hot)

20g (¾oz) butter

1 tablespoon olive oil

a few pea shoots, or little watercress sprigs (optional)

½ lemon

sea salt flakes and freshly ground black pepper

For the pea purée

350g (12oz) frozen peas

10 large mint leaves

25g (1oz) butter

50ml (3½ tablespoons) white wine

50ml (3½ tablespoons) water

Rinse the scallops well under cold water, removing any black bits with a knife and scraping away the white side muscle. Some people prefer to remove the orange roe from the scallops, but I think this is a waste so leave it on. Pat dry with kitchen paper or a clean tea towel, season with a little salt and pepper and set aside.

Prepare your chorizo. Remove the skin and then chop into chunks, each just under 1cm (½ inch). Set aside.

To make the pea purée, put the peas, mint leaves, butter, wine and water in a saucepan. Season with a little salt and pepper. Cook over a medium-high heat for about 4 minutes, or until the peas are hot, stirring regularly.

Remove from the hob and blitz with a stick blender (a high-powered blender also works well, if you have one) to make a creamy purée. Adjust the seasoning if needed. Keep the purée warm over a very low heat, stirring occasionally.

To cook the scallops, melt the butter with the olive oil in a large frying pan and cook the chorizo over a medium heat for 1–2 minutes, stirring until it begins to release its smoky red oil.

Push the chorizo to the side of the pan, increase the heat to high and add the scallops. You need to cook them for about 45 seconds on each side only, until browned. Stir the chorizo every now and then as the scallops cook, to make sure the pieces don't burn.

Divide the pea purée between 6 warmed plates and place on the scallops. Scatter with the cooked chorizo, add a few pea shoots or watercress sprigs if you like, and squeeze over a little lemon juice. Season with pepper and serve.

Smoked haddock gratin

In the midst of lockdown, we created an online cook-your-own five-course feast as part of the Wells Food Festival. We worked in collaboration with five great chefs and were joined on the night by more than 2,000 people, all cooking along at home as we live-streamed the chefs working in their home kitchens. One of the chefs we worked with that night was my friend (and food god) Henry Harris, originally of Racine fame and now back in his own kitchen at the incredible Bouchon Racine. I was a little nervous when Henry said he'd like to create the starter for our feast. A few years before, I'd organised a special lunch cooked by Henry for a gathering of foodie friends and he kicked off with some deep-fried calf's brains: delicious, but at the challenging end of eating for some. Of course I needn't have worried. Henry got things spot-on for the festival with his delicious and wonderfully simple smoked haddock gratin recipe. I reckon I now cook this at least once a month and he also inspired us to create our own version at work.

Feeds 6

Preparation time: 10 minutes

Cooking time: 15 minutes

400g (14oz) young spinach, any tough stalks removed, or baby spinach

500g (1lb 2oz) skinless smoked haddock fillets

400g (14oz) crème fraîche (I use Isigny Sainte-Mère)

50g (1¾oz) Parmesan, finely grated

freshly ground black pepper

crusty bread, to serve

Preheat the grill to hot.

Put the spinach in a large saucepan with 1 tablespoon water, cover and cook over a medium heat for 5 minutes, or until soft and wilted, stirring halfway through. Meanwhile, chop the smoked haddock into large chunks.

Drain the spinach thoroughly using a sieve or colander and squeeze out any excess water.

Mix the smoked haddock pieces in a mixing bowl with the crème fraîche and add twist or so of black pepper.

Now take 6 ramekins (ideally large and flattish) and fill each with a base layer of cooked spinach. Spoon the smoked haddock and crème fraîche mixture on top, then sprinkle over the grated Parmesan. Finish off with a generous grind or so of black pepper. Put on a baking tray.

Place the ramekins under the hot grill for 10–12 minutes, or until the filling is hot and the fish is cooked; the exact timing will depend on the size and depth of your dish. You should be able to see the crème fraîche is bubbling and the Parmesan is browning.

Stand for 5 minutes, then serve with crusty bread.

Charlie's tip The ceramic pots that come with my pie range work very well to make this dish in.

Boudin noir & caramelised apple

The problem with black pudding is that too many people have preconceptions of what it is and have decided they are not going to like it, without even having a taste. My way of getting around this is to mention it – casually – using the more sophisticated-sounding French 'boudin noir'. When buying black pudding, it's important to find a good one. In Ireland, there's never a shortage of choice in most supermarkets (my go-to being the Clonakilty brand), but it can be harder to find a good pud in the UK. If you have a good local butcher, they might be able to help; otherwise, there are some great black puddings available online: try the excellent Stornoway Black Pudding, made by the MacLeod family for the last 60 years, Fruit Pig's black pudding, or for something more exotic, the Spanish version, morcilla.

Feeds 4
Preparation time: 10 minutes
Cooking time: 25 minutes

50g (1¾oz) butter, plus more if needed

100g (3½oz) bacon or pancetta lardons

2 large onions, sliced

2 garlic cloves, chopped

3 medium-small apples (total weight about 400g / 14oz)

400g (14oz) black pudding, cut into 1cm (½ inch) slices

50ml (3½ tablespoons) brandy

sea salt flakes and freshly ground black pepper

salad leaves, or leaves from a small bunch of flat leaf parsley (about 20g / ¾oz), to serve

Melt half the butter in a large frying pan and add the bacon or pancetta lardons. Fry over a medium heat for a few minutes so they start to release their fat, stirring occasionally, then add the onions and garlic and continue to cook over a medium-low heat for 7–10 minutes, stirring occasionally. You want them to start caramelising. Remove from the pan and set aside.

Core and slice the apples (no need to remove the skins).

Melt the remaining butter in the same pan. Add the slices of apple and cook for a couple of minutes on each side until caramelised, then take out of the pan and add the black pudding slices. Cook over a medium heat for about 3 minutes on each side, or until browned on the outside and hot throughout, adding a little more butter if needed.

Tip the onion mixture and apples back in the pan and carefully mix with the black pudding slices. Season to taste. Tip in the brandy and cook over a high heat for a minute or so until reduced.

Plate up, finishing off with your salad leaves or parsley.

Charlie's tip I like to use chopped celery leaves on top of this instead of parsley, if you have squeaky-fresh stalks with their green tops intact.

Mains for two, four or six

Red pepper & goats' cheese tart

A good tart is special and I love this combination of red peppers and goats' cheese. Although this filling will work well in a traditional shortcrust pastry base, there are times when fiddling around making pastry, chilling it, rolling it out and part-baking it just seem like too much work. For this quick tart, I use good-quality ready-made puff pastry sheets pressed into a baking tray. Serve with a fresh green salad.

Feeds 4

Preparation time: 20 minutes, plus cooling

Cooking time: 40 minutes

50g (1¾oz) butter

50g (3½ tablespoons) olive oil, plus more for drizzling

4 red peppers (I use Romano, but regular peppers are fine), deseeded, cut into roughly 2cm (¾ inch) chunks

2 red onions, sliced

2 garlic cloves, chopped

325g (11½oz) sheet of ready-rolled puff pastry (all-butter is best, I like Dorset Pastry), defrosted if frozen

150g (5½oz) mini goats' cheese log, crumbled

handful of thyme sprigs

sea salt flakes and freshly ground black pepper

Melt the butter with the oil in a large frying pan over a medium-low heat and fry the peppers, onions and garlic for around 15 minutes, stirring regularly. You want everything to be softened, but without browning.

Take half the cooked vegetables and blend in a food processor or blender to form a smooth, thick purée. Keep back the rest of your cooked peppers and onions for the top of the tart. Season the purée to taste with salt and pepper and leave to cool for at least 30 minutes.

Preheat the oven to 200°C/180°C fan (400°F), Gas Mark 6. Unroll the puff pastry and press into a Swiss roll tin roughly 33 x 23cm (13 x 9 inch), or similar baking tray, filling the whole tray and creating an upturned edge all the way around. Score a border about 2cm (¾ inch) in from the edge with the tip of a sharp knife.

Spread the pastry case with the purée, then top with your reserved cooked vegetables. Bake for around 15 minutes.

Take the tart out of the oven and arrange the goats' cheese on top. Finish off with a few thyme sprigs and a drizzle of olive oil. Return to the oven for a further 10 minutes, or until the pastry is puffed up and golden brown and the goats' cheese has melted.

Charlie's tip If you have bought a frozen pre-rolled puff pastry sheet, I find you can defrost these in about one hour, if you put it in a good warm spot in the kitchen.

Roast celeriac stacks with mushrooms & spinach

Celeriac is a top (and under-appreciated) vegetable and, cooked this way, it is fantastic as the base of a really substantial dish. When I make this recipe, it's pretty casual, with the cooked ingredients piled loosely on top of each other. If you want to be a bit more showy, you can use chef's rings to make neat and elegant stacks … though that is not my style at all!

Feeds 6

Preparation time: 10 minutes

Cooking time: 30 minutes

---

3 large celeriacs, peeled

50ml (3½ tablespoons) olive oil

325g (11½oz) sheet of ready-rolled puff pastry, defrosted if frozen

1 egg, lightly beaten, or milk

75g (2¾oz) butter

2 large onions, finely sliced

500g (1lb 2oz) mushrooms (a woodland mix would be nice, or whatever you have), roughly chopped

6 garlic cloves, finely chopped

200ml (7fl oz) double cream

grating of nutmeg

400g (14oz) baby spinach

2 teaspoons Dijon mustard

1½ tablespoons finely chopped tarragon leaves, or 2 tablespoons roughly chopped flat leaf parsley leaves

sea salt flakes and freshly ground black pepper

Preheat the oven to 220°C/200°C fan (425°F), Gas Mark 7. Slice the celeriacs into 2–3cm (1 inch) thick round slices – you should get 4 rounds out of each. Pour the olive oil into a small bowl, season generously with salt and pepper and use it to brush both sides of each celeriac slice. Place the celeriac slices on a large baking tray and cook in the oven for 30 minutes, turning them after about 15 minutes. You want to end up with soft celeriac that is patched with brown on both sides and soft all the way through.

Meanwhile, roll out your puff pastry and use a 10cm (4 inch) pastry cutter, or a knife around a similar-sized saucer, to cut out 6 pastry discs, roughly the same diameter as the widest piece of celeriac. Line your second baking tray with nonstick baking paper or a reusable baking liner and arrange the pastry discs on this, brushing the top of each with beaten egg or milk. This tray will join the celeriac when you turn it over (the pastry needs about 15 minutes to cook: worth setting a timer).

Meanwhile, melt the butter in a large frying pan, add the onions with some salt and pepper and cook over a medium-high heat until soft, stirring occasionally. Add the mushrooms and garlic and cook for about 10 minutes, or until the mushrooms give out their juices.

Add the cream and nutmeg (always good with both cream and spinach), then add the spinach in 2–3 batches, covering the pan after each addition, so it wilts down into the mixture, then mix into the mushrooms. Let the pan bubble away without a lid until the spinach is wilted and the cream slightly reduced. Stir in the mustard and chopped tarragon or parsley and season with salt and pepper.

You now need to assemble your cooked components. On each plate (ideally warmed) put a celeriac slice, then a generous dollop of your mushroom and spinach mixture, then another celeriac slice, then a little more sauce and finish off each 'stack' with a cooked pastry disc. Serve immediately.

Shakshuka

Originally a North African dish from the Maghreb, Shakshuka has become increasingly popular in recent years. I've enjoyed it as a breakfast or brunch dish – most memorably at the lovely Riad El Fenn in Marrakech. It's fantastically versatile, and perfect for eating more veg or when there's a vegetarian or two at your table.

Feeds 4

Preparation time: 10 minutes

Cooking time: 30 minutes

3–4 tablespoons olive oil

2 medium-small red onions, finely sliced

3 red peppers, deseeded and cut into chunks

3 garlic cloves, finely chopped

1 green chilli, finely chopped

2 heaped teaspoons smoked paprika (hot or sweet, as you like), plus more to serve

2 heaped teaspoons ground cumin

3 tablespoons tomato purée

2 x 400g (14oz) cans of chopped tomatoes

8 large eggs

chopped parsley leaves

sea salt flakes and freshly ground black pepper

To serve

Greek yogurt

toasted wholemeal pittas

Heat 3 tablespoons of the olive oil in a large, deep frying pan (or sauté pan or casserole dish), which has a tight-fitting lid, and gently cook the onions, peppers, garlic and chilli over a medium heat for 15 minutes, or until softened and beginning to brown, stirring occasionally.

Add a little more oil, then the smoked paprika, cumin and a generous pinch of salt and pepper. Cook for 1–2 minutes, stirring. Add the tomato purée to your now cooked and spiced vegetables, give a good stir or so, then tip in both cans of chopped tomatoes. Stir and cook over a medium heat for 5 minutes, stirring regularly.

Now create 8 small dips in the sauce for each egg so that they remain separate. Break each egg into a dip, cover the pan with a tight-fitting lid and cook over a low heat for 6–8 minutes, depending on how well cooked you like your eggs.

Once the eggs are cooked, add another twist of pepper, a further sprinkle of smoked paprika and finally, chopped parsley on top. Accompany with dollops of Greek yogurt drizzled with olive oil and serve with toasted wholemeal pittas.

Risotto with chanterelles & butternut squash

There is something wonderfully satisfying about making risotto. Good risotto needs constant stirring, so pick a time when you are happy to stand at the stove for 30 minutes. It may be for a good one-to-one chat with someone, or perhaps to listen to that music you like that everyone else isn't so sure about.

Chanterelles – or girolles, if you prefer – are a favourite mushroom and, in certain places (one, fortunately being near our house), are prolific at the end of August and beginning of September. Going out hunting for chanterelles is itself a great way to spend a couple of hours. The subsequent time spent carefully brushing them, then perhaps drying a few for use later, is an enjoyably contemplative activity that, for me, is both a harbinger of autumn and an opportunity to reflect on a summer enjoyed. My recipe has been perfected by my youngest son, Miley. Not only is he a chanterelle-hunter extraordinaire, but he significantly improved my old recipe with the idea of making half the squash into a purée to stir into the risotto. This makes both the flavour and the look of the dish even better. Swap the butternut squash for beetroot if you want to have a bit of fun and create a visually stunning dish. Whether making a purée or leaving the vegetables in pieces, I always cook my base risotto and the flavouring separately, largely so I can cook a bit more risotto than I need, to ensure I have some leftovers to make arancini the following day (see page 26). Serve with a nice green salad.

Feeds 6 generously (or with leftovers for arancini, see page 26)

Preparation time: 15 minutes

Cooking time: 30 minutes

2 large onions, finely chopped

100g (3½oz) butter

2 butternut squash (total weight about 2kg / 4lb 8oz), peeled, deseeded and cut into 2cm (¾ inch) chunks

1 tablespoon olive oil, plus more for drizzling

500g (1lb 2oz) arborio rice

½ bottle (375ml / 13fl oz) inexpensive white wine

1.5 litres (2½ pints) hot chicken stock, or vegetable stock, either fresh or made with 2 stock cubes

4 tablespoons double cream

50g (1¾oz) Parmesan, shaved using a veg peeler

sea salt flakes and freshly ground black pepper

For the chanterelles

50g (1¾oz) butter

200g (7oz) fresh chanterelles, brushed or cleaned, or 100g (3½oz) dried chanterelles rehydrated in 100ml (3½fl oz) hot water

2 garlic cloves, crushed

leaves from ½ bunch of flat leaf parsley (about 15g / ½oz), chopped

To kick off your risotto, cook the onions in the butter in a large saucepan until nicely softened (5–10 minutes over a medium-low heat). Preheat the oven to 200°C/180°C fan (400°F), Gas Mark 6.

Meanwhile, put your prepared butternut squash on a baking tray, drizzle with the tablespoon of olive oil, season with salt and pepper and cook in the hot oven for about 20 minutes, or until tender. I'd recommend putting on a timer if you have it, as it's all too easy to forget about them as you slip into your stirring risotto routine below …

Once the onions are cooked sufficiently, tip in the rice, crank up the heat to high, stir the rice with the onions, then pour in the white wine. Stir until all the wine has been absorbed.

Now reduce the heat and add the stock a ladle at a time, stirring as you go (I keep my stock simmering on a low heat next to the risotto pan). Each time the stock is absorbed by the rice, add another ladleful. Continue until the rice tastes cooked, but still retains a modicum of bite right at the centre of the grains.

In between stirring your risotto, you can start cooking your chanterelles. Melt the butter in a large frying pan, add the chanterelles, garlic and parsley, season with salt and pepper and cook over a medium-high heat for 3 minutes.

When your butternut squash timer goes off, remove it from the oven and add half to your cooked chanterelles. Find a small jug or mixing bowl and use a stick blender to combine the remaining squash with the cream until you have a very smooth paste. You can't blend this purée too much, so give it a little longer than you think you need; I add the squash and cream to my jug in several batches to get an even consistency. Pour in a little water, if the purée becomes too thick.

Stir your butternut purée into the cooked rice and the whole risotto will turn a wonderful orange colour.

Just before serving, top with Parmesan shavings and a drizzle of olive oil or an extra knob of butter. Serve topped with the remaining butternut squash chunks and chanterelles.

Penne with parmesan, spinach & courgette

Inspired by the great restaurateur Antonio Carluccio, this fantastic pasta dish makes a special vegetarian main course and is a celebration of Parmesan – overall the most versatile and delicious cheese and every cook's friend. You still find a version of this dish on Carluccio's menu more than 20 years after it was devised. An anchovy or two give a little more depth to the sauce, but this is entirely optional.

Feeds 6
Preparation time: 30 minutes
Cooking time: 30 minutes

For the spinach balls

500g (1lb 2oz) baby spinach

100ml (3½fl oz) water

1 garlic clove, crushed

grating of nutmeg

pinch of chilli flakes

100g (3½oz) Parmesan, finely grated

2 eggs, lightly beaten

70g (2½oz) dried white breadcrumbs

100ml (3½fl oz) olive oil

sea salt flakes and freshly ground black pepper

For the pasta and sauce

500g (1lb 2oz) penne

50g (1¾oz) butter

3 tablespoons olive oil

5 garlic cloves, finely chopped

½ teaspoon chilli flakes, or to taste

6 good anchovies in oil, roughly chopped (optional, I like Ortiz)

2 large or 3 medium courgettes (total weight 600g / 1lb 5oz), coarsely grated

200g (7oz) baby spinach

2 tablespoons baby capers

300ml (½ pint) double cream

150g (5½oz) Parmesan, finely grated

finely grated zest of ½ lemon and juice of 1 lemon

First, you need to make the spinach balls. Put the spinach in a large saucepan over a medium-high heat with the measured water. Cook with a lid on for a minute or so, until it starts to wilt, then stir around and continue until cooked. Drain in a sieve, using a wooden spoon to press out as much water as possible. Give the spinach an extra squeeze with your hands, put on a work surface and roughly chop.

Put the spinach in a large mixing bowl with the garlic, nutmeg, chilli, Parmesan and eggs and then season with salt and pepper. Add most of the breadcrumbs to the mix and then try and create a small ball from the mixture: if it's too loose, add a few more breadcrumbs, until you achieve the right consistency. Form the mixture into balls between the size of a hazelnut and a walnut.

Heat the olive oil in a large frying pan and shallow-fry the spinach balls until brown, turning occasionally. Once they are all cooked, set aside, ideally keeping them somewhere warm.

Boil your penne in large pan of salted boiling water according to the packet instructions until al dente, then drain.

In the meantime, in your large frying pan, melt the butter, add the olive oil, then fry the garlic, chilli and anchovies, if using, for a minute. Add the grated courgettes and cook for a further 4–5 minutes, stirring as you go, or until the courgettes have softened and almost melted into a sauce.

Add the spinach and capers and cook until the spinach has wilted, stirring occasionally. Add the cream and four-fifths of the Parmesan and cook for a minute, then finally add the lemon zest and a good grinding of pepper. Bubble the sauce for another minute or so until it is reduced, then tip in the cooked pasta and give the whole lot a really good stir. Taste and adjust the seasoning if necessary.

Serve in large bowls, scatter over the warm spinach balls, then finish things off with the rest of the Parmesan and the lemon juice.

Charlie's tip Instead of adding the capers to the courgette sauce, you can fry them briefly and sprinkle them over the pasta at the end.

Gnocchi with pesto, chicory & bacon

At Charlie Bigham's, we are keen to foster an environment where we can have a bit of fun with food and learn different skills, so our chefs run masterclasses that anyone can come along to. One of my favourites has been by one of our ex-chefs, Dan, on 'how to make gnocchi'. Making gnocchi is a lot of fun and not too difficult. They are a wonderfully versatile base to many a dish, including this classic made with homemade pesto and a few wilted chicory leaves to finish things off.

Feeds 6

Preparation time: 1 hour

Cooking time: 30 minutes

1kg (2lb 4oz) floury potatoes, such as Maris Piper

2 large eggs

up to 300g (10½oz) '00' or pasta flour, plus more to dust

1–2 tablespoons extra virgin olive oil

150g (5½oz) bacon lardons

2 heads of red chicory, or radicchio, trimmed and roughly sliced

sea salt flakes and freshly ground black pepper

For the pesto

1 garlic clove

100ml (3½fl oz) extra virgin olive oil

50g (1¾oz) basil leaves

40g (1½oz) toasted pine nuts

40g (1½oz) Parmesan, finely grated

Peel the potatoes, cut into even-sized chunks and simmer in a large saucepan of salted water until tender but not falling apart. Drain well, then push the potatoes through a ricer or mouli into a large mixing bowl: this is important, as you need a very smooth mash, so just using a regular potato masher won't do the trick. You may even want to put the potatoes through the ricer or mouli for a second time, to achieve a really smooth, lump-free consistency. Leave until cool enough to handle.

Create a small well in the centre of the mash and crack in the eggs. Add a small amount of flour and a generous pinch of salt and begin to mix; you need to do this with your hands. Continue adding flour until you have a nice dough. If you don't need to use all the flour, that's fine.

Divide your dough into 4 large lumps and roll the first out into a long sausage – about the circumference of a wine cork – on a large well-floured work surface. Cut into short lengths (a thumb joint or so), then lightly press a fork into each. Keep your gnocchi well-floured and lay them on a floured board with a tea towel over them, ready for cooking. Repeat to form all the gnocchi.

To make your pesto, put the garlic and olive oil into a food processor or blender and blitz until the garlic has broken down, then add the basil, pine nuts and grated Parmesan. Blend, adding salt and pepper, to taste.

Now cook your gnocchi. Add roughly one-quarter at a time to a large saucepan of salted boiling water, wait until they float to the surface, then cook for about 1 minute more. Remove with a slotted spoon and place in a colander. Toss with a little olive oil so they don't stick together.

In a large, deep nonstick frying pan, heat a little olive oil and cook the bacon lardons until crispy. Then add the gnocchi and cook for 2–4 minutes, until beginning to turn golden. Finally, stir in your lovely fresh pesto and finish by adding the sliced chicory, stirring until it wilts in the pan.

Dynamite broth with salmon

Running a food business for more than 25 years, I've been lucky to work with people who have shaped the tastes of the nation for a generation, such as Julian Metcalfe, founder of Pret A Manger, and Itsu, the wonderful Asian restaurant chain. I helped Julian by making Itsu's sauce-of-all-sauces, the incredible 'Dynamite Broth'. This recipe takes inspiration from that broth, without replicating it precisely, which would be too complicated ... and reveal too many secrets!

If needed, two useful online places for some of the ingredients such as the katsuobushi (bonito flakes) are japancentre.com and souschef.co.uk.

Feeds 6

Preparation time: 30 minutes

Cooking time: 30 minutes

---

1 onion, finely sliced

2 slender leeks, finely sliced

2 carrots, sliced into matchsticks

1 large red pepper, finely sliced

4 heads of pak choi, chopped

750g (1lb 10oz) salmon fillet,
or 6 x 125g / 4½oz salmon steaks

2 teaspoons sunflower oil

450g (1lb) udon or egg noodles

20g (¾oz) coriander leaves

dark soy sauce

sriracha sauce (optional)

sea salt flakes and freshly ground
black pepper

lime wedges, to serve

For the broth

40g (1½oz) root ginger,
finely grated

4 garlic cloves, quartered

1 tablespoon sunflower oil

5 lime leaves, ideally fresh

200ml (7fl oz) coconut milk

150g (5½oz) white miso paste

20g (¾oz) katsuobushi
(bonito flakes)

2½ tablespoons mirin

1 tablespoon tamarind paste

1.5 litres (2¾ pints) water

First, make the broth. In a very large saucepan or flameproof casserole, briefly fry the ginger and garlic in the sunflower oil over a medium heat, stirring often. Add to a blender along with the rest of the broth ingredients, except the water. Blend together well: you want a thick, uniform paste.

Return to the pan, add the measured water and bring to the boil, then reduce the heat to a low simmer and cook for about 20 minutes.

Pass the broth through a sieve, then return it to the pan.

Add the prepared vegetables to the hot broth and simmer for 5 minutes.

Meanwhile, cook the salmon and noodles. Put the salmon skin-side down into a cold frying pan with the sunflower oil, turn the heat to medium and cook for around 4 minutes, then turn over and cook for about 3 minutes, or until just cooked through (this method means you get a nice crisp skin).

Cook your noodles according to the packet instructions, then drain and divide between 6 large serving bowls.

Serve the broth and vegetables over the noodles and place a piece of salmon on top of each. Sprinkle with chopped coriander and drizzle with a few drops of soy sauce and perhaps a squirt of spicy sriracha. Serve lime wedges on the side.

Charlie's tip This recipe also works really well if you replace the salmon with boneless chicken thighs – I cook mine on a griddle pan.

Sweet potato, paneer & okra curry

It's always good to have a vegetarian curry up your sleeve and this is a family favourite. It's my celebration of three ingredients – paneer, okra and sweet potato – that are now pretty readily available in the UK, but don't get the airtime they deserve. All are delicious in their own right but are even better when combined. The resulting curry goes down well with vegetarians and meat-eaters alike and is an inexpensive way to feed a lot of people, if you want to scale up the recipe. It's fun to serve your curry with some paratha (surprisingly easy to make, or you can buy them frozen), a bowl of yogurt raita and a jar of top-quality mango chutney, the wonderful Geeta's being my favourite. I've found this recipe works much better if you cook the main components separately and combine them at the end, ideally about 15 minutes before you are ready to eat: a little more washing up, but definitely worth it.

Feeds 6

Preparation time: 20 minutes

Cooking time: 30–40 minutes

---

3 large sweet potatoes (total weight about 725g / 1lb 9oz), peeled and cut into large chunks

6 tablespoons olive oil, or sunflower oil

2 x 250g (9oz) packs of paneer cheese, cut into roughly 2.5cm (1 inch) chunks

300g (10½oz) okra, rinsed and trimmed

2 large onions, finely sliced

2 garlic cloves, finely grated

25g (1oz) root ginger, peeled and finely grated, or 3 teaspoons ground ginger

1 teaspoon chilli flakes, or 1 fresh red chilli, finely chopped

2 teaspoons ground turmeric

1 teaspoon paprika

50g (1¾oz) tomato purée

2 x 400ml (14fl oz) cans of coconut milk

1 teaspoon sea salt flakes

big handful of coriander leaves, roughly chopped, to serve (optional)

Preheat the oven to 220°C/200°C fan (425°F), Gas Mark 7. Tip your sweet potatoes on to a large baking tray, drizzle with 1 tablespoon of the oil, toss well and roast for 20 minutes or so, until starting to brown nicely. Set aside.

Heat 2 tablespoons more oil in a large frying pan and cook the paneer chunks for 4–5 minutes, turning occasionally; you want them to start to brown nicely but not burn. (You may need to do this in 2 batches.) Lift out with a slotted spoon onto a plate lined with kitchen paper, to blot off excess oil. Fry the okra in the same frying pan for a few minutes, or until golden. Set it aside.

For your curry sauce, pour 2 tablespoons of the oil into a large saucepan or a wide-based flameproof shallow casserole and fry the onions over a medium-low heat for 5 minutes, stirring regularly, until softened and beginning to brown. Add the final 1 tablespoon of the oil, the garlic, ginger, chilli, turmeric and paprika and cook for a further 4–5 minutes, stirring.

Next add the tomato purée, coconut milk and salt, stir well and bring to a gentle simmer. Cook for 5 minutes, until everything is nicely combined and the pot is bubbling gently, then add the sweet potatoes, paneer and okra to the pan and return to a simmer.

Continue cooking for about 10 minutes. You don't want to cook the okra for more than about 10 minutes, so, if you want, hold back on adding them until you are close to being ready to serve.

Finish the curry with a generous sprinkling of chopped coriander, if you like, and serve.

Thai red prawn curry

We make a special Thai Red Chicken Curry at Charlie Bigham's, one of our bestselling dishes. I've taken all the lessons learned from that recipe, made a few small tweaks and switched the chicken for prawns. At its heart are the classic flavours of lime leaves, lemongrass and Thai basil. As for the prawns, I always recommend buying them raw and am happy to use frozen, which are often better quality as well as much easier to find. You could just use king prawns, but some sumptuous Scottish langoustines make the dish taste fantastic and look incredible. Scotland has the best langoustines in the world and I always think it's a minor food crime that so many are made into very average scampi. Give some a good home in this delicious curry instead!

Feeds 6

Preparation time: 10 minutes

Cooking time: 35–40 minutes

---

sunflower oil

3 onions, sliced

100g (3½oz) Thai red curry paste (I use Thai Taste)

1–2 red chillies, deseeded and finely chopped (optional, to taste)

25ml (1fl oz / 1½ tablespoons) fish sauce (I use Red Boat)

50g (1¾oz) raw cane sugar, or Demerara sugar

2 x 400ml (14fl oz) cans of coconut milk

2½ limes, plus extra lime wedges to serve

5–7 lime leaves (dried are fine)

1 lemongrass stalk, trimmed, peeled and bashed with a rolling pin or pestle

½ small bunch of Thai basil (about 15g / ½oz)

20g (¾oz) butter

350g (12oz) frozen langoustines in their shells (about 6–7)

400g (14oz) frozen raw peeled king prawns (about 25)

100g (3½oz) frozen edamame beans

leaves from a small bunch of coriander (about 20g / ¾oz), chopped

sticky rice, to serve

Heat a glug of oil in a large frying pan or casserole dish and cook the onions over a medium-low heat until softened (10–15 minutes).

Stir in the curry paste, three-quarters of the red chillies, if using, the fish sauce and sugar and cook for a further few minutes.

Add the coconut milk, the juice of 2 limes, the lime leaves, lemongrass stalk and half the Thai basil and cook over a medium-low heat for around 20 minutes, stirring regularly.

Meanwhile, melt the butter with a little more oil in a griddle pan or frying pan and cook the langoustines over a high heat for 4 minutes, turning halfway, then add to your curry.

Reduce the heat to low, add the frozen prawns and cook for a final 5 minutes, or until hot and the prawns are cooked, stirring in the edamame beans for the last 2 minutes and cooking until they defrost.

Scatter with the rest of the red chillies, if using, the coriander, the rest of the Thai basil and a squeeze of lime juice. Serve with sticky rice and lime wedges on the side.

Charlie's tips

- As an alternative to prawns, chop 8–10 boneless chicken thighs into large pieces and add to the curry after it has simmered for 15–20 minutes. Cook for about 15 minutes, or until cooked through, adding the edamame beans at the end.
- You can cook the sauce in advance up to the stage when you want to add the prawns, then reheat it and add them just before serving.

Monkfish with pancetta & romesco sauce

I love monkfish: definitely one of the ugliest fish around, but also tasty. It is a relatively easy fish to cook for large numbers, so good for a dinner party (and we had a version of this dish for our wedding feast). The fish is lifted by a slice of pancetta and wonderfully complemented by a classic Romesco sauce. This vibrantly piquant nut-thickened sauce from Catalonia is also tasty with chicken, lamb, other seafood and vegetarian dishes, such as chargrilled vegetables and grilled halloumi.

Feeds 6

Preparation time: 20 minutes

Cooking time: 30–35 minutes

3 tablespoons olive oil

6 x 150g (5½oz) skinless monkfish tail portions, or other white fish fillets such as haddock

6 thin slices of pancetta

juice of 1 lemon, plus extra lemon wedges to serve

small handful of thyme sprigs

For the sauce

2 large red peppers, or 200g (7oz) roasted red peppers in a jar, drained

150g (5½oz) blanched almonds

2 garlic cloves, quartered

1 tablespoon lemon juice

2 teaspoons sweet smoked paprika

½ teaspoon sea salt flakes

75ml (2¾fl oz / 5 tablespoons) extra virgin olive oil, plus more if needed

freshly ground black pepper

First, make the Romesco sauce. If you are cooking your own red peppers, you can do this in a few ways. Either put them on a baking tray and place under a hot grill for 10–15 minutes, turning regularly, until the skins are blackened and blistered, or place on the flame of a gas hob, watch carefully and turn regularly with tongs. Transfer the peppers to a bowl, cover with a plate and leave for 10 minutes, or until the skins have loosened and the peppers are cool enough to handle. Scrape off all the blackened skin, cut the peppers in half and deseed.

Put the peppers in a food processor or blender and add the almonds, garlic, lemon juice, smoked paprika, salt and half the oil. Blitz until the mixture forms a paste, then add the remaining oil and blitz again, adding a little extra oil if the sauce is a little stiff. Taste and adjust the seasoning with salt and pepper. Set aside.

Preheat the oven to 200°C/180°C fan (400°F), Gas Mark 6. Drizzle a little of the olive oil over a large baking tray or roasting tin. Pat the monkfish portions dry with kitchen paper. Place on the tray, season with salt and pepper and top each fillet with a slice of pancetta.

Drizzle the fish with the rest of the olive oil and sprinkle with the lemon juice. Scatter thyme over the top and season with pepper. Bake for around 20 minutes, or until the fish is cooked and the pancetta is beginning to crisp.

Serve on hot plates (always important the plates are hot with fish), putting a generous dollop of Romesco sauce on the plate with the fish on top and lemon wedges on the side.

Smoky butter beans with hake

We all need to eat more beans: they are nutritious and delicious! You can, of course, cook your own beans from scratch, but I've found there are a couple of companies that do all the hard work for you, my favourite being Bold Bean Co set up by the talented Amelia Christie-Miller. Increasingly available in supermarkets, you will also find her lovely beans online. For this recipe, I've topped the beans with a perfect piece of hake, perhaps a little less popular than its close cousin cod, but just as good in my view. Serve with crusty bread and a lightly dressed salad in summer, or freshly cooked greens in winter.

Feeds 4

Preparation time: 10 minutes

Cooking time: 30 minutes

1½ tablespoons olive oil

4 x 150–200g (5½–7oz) hake fillets, or other white fish fillets

extra virgin olive oil

juice of ½ lemon

finely chopped flat leaf parsley leaves

crusty bread, to serve

For the beans

4 tablespoons olive oil

2 large onions, sliced

2 celery sticks, finely sliced

3 large garlic cloves, finely chopped

2 teaspoons sweet smoked paprika

400g (14oz) can of chopped tomatoes

200g (7oz) tomato passata

700g (1lb 9oz) jar of large or queen butter beans (Bold Bean Co are particularly good)

sea salt flakes and freshly ground black pepper

Start by making the beans. Heat 3 tablespoons of the oil in a large shallow casserole, sauté pan or deep frying pan with a lid and fry the onions and celery gently for 10 minutes, or until softened and beginning to brown, stirring regularly. Add the garlic and cook for 3 minutes more, stirring frequently.

Pour the rest of the oil into the pan and add the paprika. Cook for a minute, stirring constantly. Next add the tomatoes, passata and the beans with all their liquid. Season with lots of pepper; you shouldn't need extra salt as the beany liquid will already be fairly salty. Bring to a gentle simmer and cook for 10 minutes, stirring regularly.

Meanwhile, place a frying pan over a medium-high heat, add the 1½ tablespoons oil and then the fish, skin-side down. Season with salt and pepper and cook for 2 minutes. Carefully flip the fish over, add a dash more oil and cook for a further 4 minutes, or until pale golden and almost cooked through.

Lift the fish gently on to the cooked beans, cover the pan with a lid and simmer gently for a further 4–5 minutes, or until the fish is just cooked: it should be firm but ready to flake into large pieces if prodded. Take off the heat, drizzle with a little extra virgin olive oil, squeeze over the lemon juice and scatter lots of chopped parsley on top. Serve with crusty bread.

Griddled squid with a tomato-pepper salsa

Squid is a relatively inexpensive and readily available seafood. Plenty is caught off the UK coast, but for some reason we don't eat a lot of it. If you can, buy it fresh – there are several good online suppliers of all things fishy – but otherwise you should find it frozen in most supermarkets (avoid buying pre-cut squid rings, as you need whole squid for this dish). This is a simple, quick, zingy recipe that makes a great summer lunch or light dinner. I'm not too fussy about what goes into my salsa – though for me tomatoes are essential – it's usually a case of looking at what's in the fridge, so feel free to mix it up a bit, trying cucumber and different-coloured peppers.

Feeds 4

Preparation time: 30 minutes

Cooking time: 5 minutes

500g (1lb 2oz) squid
(3–4 medium-large squid)

juice of 1 lemon

leaves from a bushy thyme or oregano sprig, finely chopped

2 garlic cloves, crushed

3 tablespoons olive oil

sea salt flakes and freshly ground black pepper

For the salsa

2 tomatoes, chopped

1 small red onion, finely chopped

1 red pepper, deseeded and finely chopped

1 green pepper, or ½ cucumber, or 1 green tomato, deseeded and finely chopped

2 garlic cloves, finely chopped

½ bunch of coriander
(about 15g / ½oz), leaves
and stalks finely chopped

juice of 2 large limes

4 tablespoons extra virgin olive oil

1 teaspoon runny honey

good shake of Tabasco sauce
(I have a penchant for the green variety)

½–1 green or red chilli, deseeded and finely chopped (optional)

Prepare the squid (if the fishmonger hasn't already done this). Remove the insides, including the quill (the stiff transparent bone-like material), then peel off the mottled purple skin. Slice the tubes down the side to open them up.

Score each flattened tube on the inside with a cross-hatch, using a sharp knife, scraping away any membrane as you go. Cut into large square pieces.

Once all your squid is prepared, place in a large non-metallic bowl with its tentacles and add the lemon juice, herbs, garlic, olive oil and a generous pinch of salt and pepper.

To make your salsa, put everything in a separate non-metallic bowl, adding as much or as little Tabasco and chilli as you like, if using. Season with a little salt.

To cook your squid, preheat your griddle pan until searing hot: this is very important. Brush off the marinade ingredients and then cook the squid for around 2 minutes on each side, pressing it down with a metal spatula if it starts to curl up. It should look nicely charred when ready.

Serve the squid with a generous amount of the salsa alongside. I like this as part of a mezze, or with leaves, for a light supper. For a more substantial supper, I serve it with tagliatelle dressed in olive oil, lemon zest and basil, perhaps with a few drops of balsamic vinegar on each plate for a final flourish.

Mussels with chorizo & garlic

I can heartily recommend this as an alternative to the equally lovely Moules Marinière (see page 123). The recipe comes from Galicia, one of the great gastronomic regions of the world. The restaurants of San Sebastían are famous and have been awarded an impressive array of Michelin stars, but one of my favourite foodie towns in Galicia is La Coruña – a veritable seafood mecca – where I once spent a memorable 24 hours of eating before embarking on a week-long sailing trip into the Atlantic. The mussels were particularly memorable, with brighter orange flesh and a slightly sweeter flavour than the more northern blue mussel we usually eat in the UK. This recipe works well with both types.

Feeds 6
Preparation time: 20 minutes
Cooking time: 35 minutes

___

500ml (18fl oz) water

2kg (4lb 8oz) fresh, live mussels, prepared (see tip)

75g (2¾oz) butter

4 tablespoons olive oil

2 large onions, sliced

1 red pepper, deseeded and cut into roughly 1cm (½ inch) chunks

2 yellow or orange peppers, deseeded and cut into roughly 1cm (½ inch) chunks

8 garlic cloves, finely chopped

350g (12oz) cooking chorizo, skinned and cut into roughly 1cm (½ inch) chunks

5 teaspoons sweet smoked paprika

2 teaspoons chilli flakes, or 1 fresh red chilli, finely chopped

pinch of saffron threads (optional)

2 x 400g (14oz) cans of chopped tomatoes

200ml (7fl oz) white wine

2 rosemary sprigs

2 bay leaves

50ml (3½ tablespoons) sherry vinegar

finely grated zest and juice of 1 lemon

chopped parsley leaves

sea salt flakes and freshly ground black pepper

crusty bread, to serve

Pour the water into a large saucepan and bring to the boil. Add the mussels, cover and steam for around 5 minutes, so that they open (you will need to stir to turn them a little after about 3 minutes, to ensure those at the top open too). Drain in a large colander and leave to cool slightly. Remove the mussels from their shells, discarding any that haven't opened, and set aside.

Melt the butter with the oil in a large, deep frying pan, sauté pan or wide-based shallow casserole over a low heat. Add the onions and cook for around 5 minutes, stirring occasionally.

Add the peppers and garlic and cook for a further 5 minutes, stirring regularly. Add the chorizo, smoked paprika, chilli and saffron, if using, and cook for 3-4 minutes more, stirring.

Tip the chopped tomatoes into the pan and add the white wine, rosemary, bay and sherry vinegar. Bring to a gentle simmer and cook for a further 10 minutes, stirring every now and then.

Finally, stir in the shelled mussels, lemon zest and juice. Simmer over a low heat for around 5 minutes, or until the mussels are hot, stirring regularly. Season with salt and pepper. Before serving, scatter with chopped parsley. Serve with crusty bread.

Charlie's tip Keep mussels in the fridge and use within a day or two of buying. Pick them over, pulling off any 'beards' (the strings that hang out of the shell) and scraping off barnacles with a blunt knife. Discard any mussels that are cracked, or don't close when you tap them on the work surface, or don't open when cooked (all signs of dead shellfish).

Bashed chicken with parmesan breadcrumbs

Not a fancy or sophisticated dish, but a mighty tasty one that can be knocked up in no time. It's also great if you've got some (slightly fussy) kids around, as it tends to go down pretty well with almost everyone. The fun you can have is with the breadcrumb mix. Here I've introduced both flavour and texture with polenta, Parmesan, paprika and parsley; you can easily simplify matters by leaving out an ingredient or two.

Feeds 2 (and easy to scale up)
Preparation time: 25 minutes
Cooking time: 10 minutes

2 small skinless chicken breasts, about 150g (5½oz) each

100g (3½oz) dried white breadcrumbs

30g (1oz) polenta (any type)

40g (1½oz) Parmesan, finely grated

leaves from ½ bunch of flat leaf parsley (about 15g / ½oz), finely chopped

finely grated zest of ½ lemon

1 teaspoon paprika

1 egg

3 tablespoons light olive oil, or sunflower oil

sea salt flakes and freshly ground black pepper

To serve

2 lemon wedges

cooked green beans

cooked new potatoes

Tomato-Pepper Salsa (see page 89, optional)

Taking each chicken breast in turn, place it between 2 pieces of clingfilm, then bash repeatedly with a meat hammer or rolling pin until the chicken breast has nearly doubled in size (you want the chicken to be pretty thin).

Mix the breadcrumbs, polenta, Parmesan, parsley, lemon zest, paprika, a generous pinch of salt and 2–3 twists of pepper in a large mixing bowl. Tip half the breadcrumbs on to a plate. Break the egg into a shallow dish and whisk well.

Dip each piece of chicken first into the egg and then into the breadcrumbs, ensuring that each side of the chicken gets a decent coating. Add the rest of the breadcrumbs to the plate after the first breast is coated, then coat the second.

Heat up the oil in a large frying pan, then add the chicken. You want to cook over a medium heat for 4–5 minutes on each side until the breadcrumbs are crisp and golden brown and the chicken is cooked through. Serve with lemon wedges, green beans, new potatoes and the Tomato-Pepper Salsa.

Charlie's tips
- You can easily make these in advance and keep them in a warm oven (110°C/90°C fan (225°F), Gas Mark ¼, say) for an hour or so.
- I always have a stash of homemade dried breadcrumbs in my freezer. I dry crusts, offcuts and staling bread in a warm oven, then blitz in a food processor and tip into a sandwich bag – you can use them straight from the freezer.

Apple & walnut chicken olives

A recipe from the archives at work. Although we stopped making this dish many years ago, I still cook it at home because I enjoy the simplicity of both preparation and taste. An 'olive' is a somewhat old-fashioned term for meat wrapped around a stuffing: beef olives were a staple of the 1970s, but I've always found them disappointing – chicken thigh works much better. This stuffing is lovely and autumnal: apples, walnuts, sultanas and a generous amount of sage. Delicious with Sautéed Potatoes with Paprika and Rosemary or Parsnips with Garlic, Thyme & Honey (see pages 166 and 190) and a green vegetable such as chard, or maybe a saucy vegetable such as creamed leeks.

Feeds 4

Preparation time: 30 minutes

Cooking time: 30–40 minutes

8 skinless boneless chicken thighs

16 pancetta rashers, or thin-cut streaky bacon rashers

a little olive oil

8 sage leaves

3 tablespoons (about 50g / 1³⁄₄oz) apricot jam, to glaze

For the stuffing

1 small shallot, finely chopped

1 small apple, cored and chopped into small pieces (no need to remove the skin)

200g (7oz) minced pork

50g (1³⁄₄oz) dried white breadcrumbs

30g (1oz) walnut pieces, quite finely chopped

10g (¹⁄₄oz) sultanas

1 egg yolk

3 large sage leaves, chopped (about ³⁄₄ tablespoon chopped sage leaves)

sea salt flakes and freshly ground black pepper

Put all the ingredients for the stuffing into a mixing bowl, season with lots of salt and pepper and mix well. Line a baking sheet with nonstick baking paper or a reusable baking liner. Preheat the oven to 200°C/180°C fan (400°F), Gas Mark 6.

Lay a couple of chicken thighs flat, the side where the skin was down, on a piece of clingfilm on a work surface and put another piece of clingfilm on top. Flatten with a meat hammer or rolling pin. Repeat with the rest.

Lay 2 pancetta or bacon rashers, with a 2cm (¾ inch) space between, on a fresh piece of lightly oiled clingfilm. Put a sage leaf across them in the centre. Lay a flattened chicken thigh on top and spoon one-eighth of the stuffing in the centre. Use the clingfilm to carefully roll up the chicken around the stuffing to form an 'olive'. Turn over and place on the prepared baking sheet. Repeat with the rest of the pancetta, sage, chicken and stuffing.

Brush your olives with apricot jam and season with black pepper. Cook in the oven for 30–40 minutes, or until the chicken is cooked through and the pancetta is browning.

Charlie's tip This is a very easy recipe to scale up and can easily be prepared up to a day in advance and kept in the fridge until you are ready to cook the olives (though bring them to room temperature first).

Breton chicken with a chive mornay sauce

This recipe was one of the very first we started with at Charlie Bigham's, way back in 1996, and we reckon it has been eaten by more than half a million people! It's simple, combining the complementary flavours of chicken, bacon, leeks and cheese for a quick and easy supper.

Feeds 4–5

Preparation time: 15 minutes

Cooking time: 15 minutes

650–700g (about 1lb 8oz) chicken mini fillets, or skinless breasts

100g (3½oz) bacon lardons

juice of ½ lemon

leaves from a small bunch of flat leaf parsley (about 20g / ¾oz), chopped

300ml (½ pint) single cream

50g (1¾oz) mature Cheddar, finely grated

2 garlic cloves, finely chopped

2 teaspoons Dijon mustard

2 teaspoons cornflour

200ml (7fl oz) chicken stock, made with 1 stock cube

25g (1oz) butter, or 1 tablespoon olive oil

2 slender leeks (total weight about 300g / 10½oz), sliced into large pieces on an angle

½ small bunch of chives (about 10g / ¼oz), finely chopped

sea salt flakes and freshly ground black pepper

Chop the chicken into bite-sized pieces. Put into a large mixing bowl with the lardons, lemon juice, parsley, a little salt and generous amount of pepper. Mix thoroughly.

Make your sauce by thoroughly blitzing together the cream, cheese, garlic, mustard and cornflour in a jug or mixing bowl using a stick blender, or in a food processor. Stir in the stock.

Now melt the butter or oil in a large frying pan and add your chicken and bacon mixture. Cook over a fairly high heat for 5 minutes, stirring frequently. You want the chicken to brown a bit and the bacon to begin to crisp up.

Add the leeks to the pan, stirring them in well. Cook for a further 3–4 minutes.

Pour in the sauce, increase the heat to high and heat through, stirring frequently, for around 3 minutes, or until the sauce has reduced slightly. Sprinkle over the chives and serve.

Cajun chicken legs with mango salsa

The very first chef I worked with at my company was the wonderful and talented Spike. This was the first dish he ever cooked for me – and I've been cooking it ever since. The secret is to really work the spices into the chicken to ensure the flavours penetrate well. When balanced by a lovely fruity salsa such as this, you'll find you can handle a little more spice than your usual limit. This is delicious served with Green Beans with Hazelnuts, and Carrots with Pumpkin Seeds & a Sesame Dressing (see pages 183 and 153).

Feeds 4

Preparation time: 20 minutes

Cooking time: 40 minutes

---

3 garlic cloves

1 small onion, roughly chopped

2 tablespoons olive oil, plus more for the tray

80g (2¾oz) Cajun seasoning

4 chicken legs (whole legs, not just drumsticks)

For the salsa

1 large mango (a little unripe works best)

bunch of coriander, about 30g (1oz)

½ large red onion, very finely chopped, the finer the better

2 tablespoons extra virgin olive oil

juice of 1 lime

Tabasco sauce, or ½ red chilli, finely chopped, to taste

sea salt flakes and freshly ground black pepper

To serve

cooked plain rice

fresh green salad

Preheat the oven to 200°C/180°C fan (400°F), Gas Mark 6.

First off, you need to make your Cajun paste. Put the garlic cloves in a food processor or blender with the onion and 1 tablespoon of the olive oil and blend to a purée. Tip in three-quarters of the Cajun seasoning, add the rest of the olive oil and continue to blend. You are aiming for a thick orange paste.

Liberally smear each chicken leg all over with the paste, making sure that every bit of chicken has got its fair share. Put the chicken legs on a well-oiled large baking tray, sprinkle over the rest of the Cajun seasoning and roast for 40 minutes, or until tender and browned. Rest for a few minutes before serving.

Meanwhile, make the salsa. Peel the mango, then slice off the luscious orange flesh around the stone and finely chop it. Roughly chop the coriander stalks and leaves.

Put the red onion, mango, coriander, olive oil and lime juice in a mixing bowl and mix thoroughly. Season with salt, pepper and Tabasco or red chilli, to taste.

Serve the chicken legs with a generous dollop of the mango salsa, alongside some cooked rice and a green salad.

Chicken with ginger, cumin, honey & almonds

A great easy dish that everyone loves, this recipe takes inspiration from the wonderful flavours of the Middle East and is a regular in our house. If you've got a fair few people eating, I find some are happy with a single chicken thigh and those (like me!) who are a little greedier will eat two. It's a straightforward recipe to scale up or down and works well for a crowd, as you can leave it in a warm oven for 30 minutes or more once cooked. Delicious with Persian Rice, and Tenderstem Broccoli with Garlic & Chilli (see pages 164 and 184).

Feeds 6 generously (and easy to scale up)

Preparation time: 15 minutes

Cooking time: 50 minutes

---

3 large onions, sliced

5 tablespoons olive oil

4 garlic cloves, finely chopped

1 tablespoon ground cumin, plus 1 heaped teaspoon

1 tablespoon ground ginger, plus 1 heaped teaspoon

1 teaspoon chilli flakes (optional)

8–12 skin-on bone-in chicken thighs

juice of 1 lemon

50g (1¾oz) ground almonds

50g (1¾oz) flaked almonds

generous drizzle (about 2 tablespoons) runny honey

handful of parsley leaves, finely chopped

sea salt flakes and freshly ground black pepper

Preheat the oven to 200°C/180°C fan (400°F), Gas Mark 6.

Put the onions in a wide-based, shallow ovenproof dish and sprinkle with a couple of glugs of oil (about 4 tablespoons), the garlic, 1 tablespoon each of ground cumin and ground ginger, plus the chilli flakes, if you're after a bit of spice. Toss together, then put in the oven for 15 minutes, or until soft but not browned.

Meanwhile, drizzle 1 tablespoon of oil into a large frying pan and pan-fry the chicken thighs for around 5 minutes on each side, starting on the skin side, until nicely browned. (If cooking a larger number of thighs, you will need to fry in 2 batches, or use 2 frying pans.)

Once the onions are cooked, remove from the oven and stir lightly. Place the chicken thighs on top, skin-side up. Pour any juices from the frying pan on top of the chicken with the lemon juice. Season generously with salt, pepper and the remaining 1 heaped teaspoon each of cumin and ginger. Sprinkle the chicken with the ground almonds and return the dish to the oven for 30 minutes, or until the chicken is tender and cooked through.

Remove the dish from the oven and scatter the flaked almonds on top. Drizzle generously with honey. Return the dish to the oven for about 5 minutes, or until the almonds are lightly toasted (be careful they don't burn).

Take the finished dish from the oven and scatter liberally with chopped parsley.

Roast chicken, leek & ham pie

Everyone loves a pie. We've been making them at Charlie Bigham's for 20 years and they have something of a cult following, especially the ones we sell in individual ceramic ramekins. I know some people will say: 'Hang on a minute, but are these even pies? Surely a proper pie has pastry all around it, not just on top?' If you're a pie purist and want a pastry base, please adapt the recipe accordingly. This is one of my favourites and can easily be adjusted for that post-Christmas Day meal we are all familiar with, when you wonder what to do with the leftover turkey. For this recipe, I roast a whole chicken to ensure maximum flavour, the ham hock can be bought pre-made (it's effectively slow-cooked pulled ham), and don't scrimp on the leeks: they are key to the overall flavour.

Feeds 6 generously

Preparation time: 30 minutes

Cooking time: 1 hour, more if roasting your own chicken

---

1 large roast chicken, about 2kg (4lb 8oz), to yield about 750g (1lb 10oz) meat

4 large leeks (about 725g / 1lb 9oz), roughly chopped

100g (3½oz) butter

leaves from a few thyme sprigs

250g (9oz) ham hock meat, or other boneless ham, chopped

500g (1lb 2oz) ready-made puff pastry

plain flour, to dust

1 egg, lightly beaten

For the béchamel

50g (1¾oz) butter

50g (1¾oz) plain flour

600ml (20fl oz) milk

good grating of nutmeg

100ml (3½fl oz) double cream

150ml (¼ pint) chicken stock, either fresh or made with 1 stock cube

sea salt flakes and freshly ground white pepper, or black pepper

Pull all the roast chicken off the carcass and break up with your hands into pieces that you'd want to eat. (I recommend keeping all the skin and bones to make a good chicken stock.)

Make your béchamel. Start by melting the butter in a large saucepan, then tip in the flour and stir for about a minute so the flour is cooked. Slowly add the milk, stirring frequently to ensure there are no lumps. Add the nutmeg, pepper and cream. Keep over a low heat, stirring often, until the sauce is smooth. Stir in the stock and season, if needed, with a little salt.

In a frying pan, fry your leeks in the butter until nicely softened (6–8 minutes), adding the thyme leaves towards the end.

Now combine your chicken and leeks with the béchamel and crumble in the ham hock. Season well. Thoroughly mix and tip into a large (2-litre / 3½-pint) pie dish. Leave to cool, or cover and chill, if making in advance.

Preheat the oven to 200°C/180°C fan (400°F), Gas Mark 6.

Roll out the puff pastry on a floured work surface to the correct size to fit your pie dish, then place over the dish. Crimp around the edge with your thumb. You can score the top lightly with a small sharp knife to decorate the pie (being careful not to pierce the pastry). Finally, finish with a brush of egg wash.

Cook in the oven for 35–40 minutes, adding a little more time if your pie filling was chilled.

Duck breasts with soy-honey glaze & pak choi

We eat a lot of duck breasts at home. Much tastier than chicken and quick and easy to cook, they work well in lots of different dishes: warm salads, stir-fries, curries and of course with a classic fruity sauce, often plum or orange. This is a favourite dish for a quick no-nonsense supper – duck cooked simply with Chinese-inspired flavours, then sliced and served on a bed of pak choi, perhaps with a little nest of egg noodles or some sticky rice.

Feeds 4

Preparation time: 5 minutes

Cooking time: 15 minutes

---

4 duck breasts, trimmed of any excess fat

egg noodles or sticky rice, to serve

For the glaze

2 teaspoons tamarind paste

2 tablespoons soy sauce (Kikkoman is my favourite)

½ teaspoon Szechuan peppercorns, crushed

1 teaspoon five spice powder

pinch of ground ginger

a few grinds of pepper

1½ tablespoons runny honey

finely grated zest and juice of 1 orange

For the pak choi

500g (1lb 2oz) pak choi

1½ tablespoons toasted sesame oil

3 garlic cloves, finely chopped

1 tablespoon soy sauce

Preheat the oven to 200°C/180°C fan (400°F), Gas Mark 6. Mix all the ingredients for the glaze except the orange juice.

Chop up the pak choi stalks into equal-sized pieces and roughly chop the leaves.

Score the skin of the duck breasts across in both directions using the tip of a sharp knife, without going right down to the meat.

Place the duck breasts skin-side down in a cold ovenproof frying pan, then place over a medium heat (this will help the fat render). You need to cook them for around 7 minutes, or until the skin has browned nicely and started to crisp. Turn over and cook for a minute or so on the other side.

Take the pan off the heat and smear the glaze on the skin side. Transfer the pan to the oven for a final 5 minutes.

Take the duck out of the oven, deglaze the pan with the orange juice (stir and scrape with a wooden spoon to loosen all the stuck on bits and to combine them into the sauce) and turn the duck over in the glaze. Cover with a lid or a large heatproof plate and allow the meat to rest.

Meanwhile, stir-fry your pak choi. Heat the oil in a wok or large frying pan. Briefly fry the garlic, then add the pak choi stalks and stir-fry until nearly tender. Add the pak choi leaves and continue to stir-fry until wilted, adding the soy sauce at the end.

Uncover the duck frying pan and spoon the juices from the pan over the duck, then slice and serve on top of the wilted pak choi, with the rest of the juices. This is delicious with either egg noodles or sticky rice.

Partridge tagine

I love Middle Eastern food of all descriptions and have a special soft spot for Moroccan cooking. The exoticism of the country is manifested in its food – a wonderful fusion of strong Middle Eastern flavours, overlaid with a French culinary influence. For this recipe, I've used partridges for a tasty and elegant tagine that uses a good seasonal ingredient, found from September to December. However, you can substitute small poussins or other birds (see tip). A tagine isn't complete without couscous, so here I've stuffed it inside the partridges and ensured there's plenty of sauce to soak into the grain when you serve it.

Feeds 4

Preparation time: 15 minutes

Cooking time: 50–60 minutes

½ quantity Couscous with Apricots, Parsley & Red Onion (see page 167)

100ml (3½fl oz) olive oil

3 red onions, sliced

3 teaspoons ground cumin

2 teaspoons paprika

2 teaspoons ground turmeric

6 garlic cloves, finely chopped

40g (1½oz) root ginger, peeled and grated, or 2 teaspoons ground ginger

4 partridges, or small poussins, each no larger than 500g (1lb 2oz)

150g (5½oz) pitted dates

½ preserved lemon, seeds removed, finely chopped

finely grated zest and juice of 2 lemons

1 fresh red chilli, deseeded and finely chopped, or ½–¾ teaspoon chilli flakes

350ml (12fl oz) chicken stock, or vegetable stock

3 tablespoons runny honey

3 pinches of sumac

handful of flat leaf parsley leaves, chopped

handful of coriander, chopped

25g (1oz) shelled unsalted pistachios, roughly chopped

sea salt flakes and freshly ground black pepper

pomegranate molasses, to serve

Prepare the couscous recipe on page 167 (no cooking required and only 15 minutes work). Half the quantity is the perfect amount to stuff 4 birds, so either halve the ingredients as I suggest, or make the full amount and serve the rest alongside.

Preheat the oven to 200°C/180°C fan (400°F), Gas Mark 6.

Put the olive oil in a large shallow casserole or tagine and add the onions, cumin, paprika and turmeric. Cook in the oven for 20 minutes, stirring in the garlic and ginger after 10 minutes. It doesn't really matter if you cover them or not, but if you do, you retain a few more of their lovely juices, which is no bad thing.

Meanwhile, stuff the partridges or poussins with the couscous. You can tie the legs together with some butcher's string (sometimes I bother to do this and sometimes not).

Stir the dates and preserved lemon, lemon zest and juice and chilli into your cooked onions, then arrange the stuffed birds on top.

Pour over your stock and finally drizzle the partridges or poussins with the honey and sprinkle with the sumac. Season with salt and pepper.

Return to the oven, uncovered, and cook for around 30 minutes for slightly pink meat (my preference), or 40 minutes if you want the birds well done. (If you are cooking in a tagine this would be traditionally placed on top of some hot embers and then cooked slowly for longer.)

Once the partridges are cooked, sprinkle over the chopped parsley, coriander and pistachios before serving, finishing off with a swirl of pomegranate molasses, if you have it.

Charlie's tip If you can't get hold of partridges and are keen on something more exotic than poussins, the recipe also works well with quails or pigeons.

Beef bourguignon

As soon as I catch the first glimpse of autumn, my culinary thoughts inevitably turn to warming, slow-cooked stews. I love the summer for all its abundance and freshness, but there's something deeply comforting about cold walks, log fires, red wine and a delicious, well-cooked beef bourguignon! We make what I think is a pretty tasty recipe at Charlie Bigham's, so I thought I'd share my home version. The secret is to start with some good-quality beef: if you are going to the butcher, ask for chuck, but if you're buying in the supermarket, look out for braising steak. I recommend buying a whole piece and cutting it up at home so you have some nice chunky pieces. Delicious accompanied with Parsnips with Garlic, Thyme & Honey, and Savoy Cabbage with Chestnuts (see pages 190 and 194).

Feeds 6

Preparation time: 30 minutes

Cooking time: 2½–3 hours

1kg (2lb 4oz) braising steak

50g (1¾oz) plain flour

50g (1¾oz) butter

50ml (3½ tablespoons) olive oil

½ bottle (375ml / 13fl oz) red wine

100g (3½oz) pancetta lardons, or bacon lardons

3 red onions, cut into wedges

1 celery stick, finely chopped

5 garlic cloves, finely chopped

450g (1lb) chestnut mushrooms, quartered (no need to peel)

2 tablespoons tomato purée

3 teaspoons Dijon mustard

500ml (18fl oz) fresh beef stock

10–12 Chantenay carrots, topped but left whole, or 3 regular carrots, chopped into 6cm (2½ inch) pieces

rosemary sprig

a few thyme sprigs

2 bay leaves

170g (6oz) jar of Borettane onions (or other pearl onions) in vinegar, drained

sea salt flakes and freshly ground black pepper

small bunch of flat leaf parsley (about 20g / ¾oz), leaves roughly chopped, to serve

First you need to cut up your beef into good-sized pieces (about 7–8cm / 3 inches). Put half the flour in a mixing bowl, season well with salt and pepper and tumble the meat in this so it is well coated.

Melt the butter in a frying pan with the oil and cook the floured meat on both sides over a high heat for 5–7 minutes, or until browned – do this in two batches to avoid overcrowding the pan, putting the meat to one side once cooked. Deglaze the pan with some of the wine, scraping up the tasty bits on the bottom of the pan. Set the liquid aside with the cooked meat.

Meanwhile, start preparing your sauce. Heat the remaining butter and olive oil in a casserole dish. Add the pancetta or bacon and cook for a couple of minutes so it starts to release its fat. Add the red onions and celery and cook for 5 minutes or so, until the vegetables have softened, stirring occasionally. Add the garlic and mushrooms and cook for another 10 minutes or so, stirring occasionally. Sprinkle the rest of the flour into the pan, then stir in with the tomato purée and Dijon mustard.

As the mixture cooks, preheat the oven to 180°C/160°C fan (350°F), Gas Mark 4.

Tip in the rest of the red wine, then the beef stock and give everything a good stir before adding the carrots, herbs and drained onions. Finally, add the beef plus the pan deglazing juices.

Bring to the boil, then cover the casserole dish, put it in the oven and cook for 2–2½ hours, stirring every 30 minutes or so, until the meat is tender. You can take the lid off for 30 minutes towards the end of cooking to slightly thicken the sauce. Taste and adjust the seasoning if necessary. Finish with a scattering of parsley.

Lamb koftas

One of the joys of travelling in the Middle East is you are likely to have frequent encounters with people doing remarkable things with lamb. I've been lucky enough to have had more than my fair share of such occasions. There were the delicious spicy merguez sausages in the backstreets of Fez, the remarkable skewered fillets of lamb in Isfahan, and spending an entire day going 'to eat lamb' (and drink raku) in the Taurus mountains above Adana in south-east Turkey with my wife Claire's Turkish cousin Muti.

This recipe takes its main inspiration from the Adana kebab, the spiced lamb kebab from the city, famous throughout Turkey, but I've included a little couscous, which helps their texture, and also used my favourite Kashmiri chilli – you won't find better! These koftas are best cooked over hot coals for maximum flavour, but you can grill them as well. Either way, I recommend that you invest in some good-quality FLAT skewers. These are far better than the standard-issue round metal skewers, which mean food has a tendency to spin around, or fall off completely. In addition to the accompaniments below, you could also serve these with my Green Salad with Roast Artichokes & Avocado and some Persian Rice (see pages 154 and 164).

Feeds 4–5 / Makes 10

Preparation time: 15 minutes

Cooking time: 15 minutes

50g (1¾oz) couscous

20ml (¾fl oz / 4 teaspoons) cold water

500g (1lb 2oz) minced lamb (not too lean, if there is a choice)

1 red pepper, deseeded and very finely chopped

1 onion, very finely chopped

3 garlic cloves, crushed

leaves from ½ bunch of flat leaf parsley (about 15g / ½oz), roughly chopped

2 teaspoons ground Kashmiri chilli, or 1 teaspoon finely ground chilli flakes

1 teaspoon dried oregano

1 teaspoon ground cumin

1 teaspoon sea salt flakes

To serve

shredded red cabbage

shredded lettuce

Tzatziki (see page 180)

Roast Aubergines with Garlic & Herbs (see page 188)

Put the couscous in a small bowl and stir in the cold water. Leave to stand.

One of the characteristics of the Adana kebab is that it is made of finely minced lamb that has been almost minced to a paste. So put all the remaining ingredients (except the soaking couscous) in a stand mixer fitted with the paddle attachment, then mix for about 3 minutes to make an almost smooth paste. Crumble the couscous on top and mix for a further 1–2 minutes or until well combined.

With wetted hands, form your lamb mixture into 10 long sausages. Put a skewer through the middle of each and then squish flat. (If cooking on a flat griddle rather than a barbecue or ridged griddle pan use a spare skewer to mark horizontal lines across the kebabs.) Now they are ready for cooking.

Cook over some hot coals for about 15 minutes, turning occasionally to ensure they don't burn. Alternatively, cook on a preheated hot ridged griddle pan for 4–5 minutes on each side. Serve with shredded red cabbage and lettuce, Tzatziki and Roast Aubergines with Garlic and Herbs.

Sausage & puy lentil casserole

Inspired by a tasty lentil dish we shared in a small Parisian brasserie many moons ago, my wife Claire adapted the recipe to include good old-fashioned English bangers and it became a regular family supper. I love the nuttiness of Puy lentils and they make a wonderful rich casserole. My friend Olly at The Jolly Hog in Bristol sells a delicious range of proper sausages, which I like to use here. Delicious served with mash.

Feeds 6

Preparation time: 15 minutes

Cooking time: 1 hour 10 minutes

---

12 meaty sausages (such as The Jolly Hog Proper Porkers)

3 tablespoons olive oil

25g (1oz) butter

1 medium-large onion, finely chopped

1 large carrot, finely chopped

1 celery stick, finely chopped

1 fennel bulb, finely chopped

150g (5½oz) bacon lardons, smoked or unsmoked

4 garlic cloves, finely chopped

300g (10½oz) Puy lentils, or small green lentils

2 tablespoons balsamic vinegar

1 tablespoon Dijon mustard

bushy thyme sprig

1 litre (1¾ pints) chicken stock, or vegetable stock, either fresh or made with 1½ stock cubes

sea salt flakes and freshly ground black pepper

Fry the sausages in a large shallow casserole dish with 1 tablespoon of the olive oil over a medium heat until they are nicely browned; 5 minutes should be enough as they don't need to be cooked all the way through. Lift the sausages out and set aside.

In the same pan, add the remaining oil and the butter, onion, carrot, celery and fennel. Cook over a low heat for about 10 minutes, stirring occasionally. Once the vegetables have softened well, add the bacon lardons and garlic and fry for a further 5 minutes, stirring regularly.

Preheat the oven to 200°C/180°C fan (400°F), Gas Mark 6.

Add the lentils, balsamic vinegar, mustard, thyme, a generous pinch of salt and lots of pepper. Stir in the sausages and stock and bring to the boil. Cover with a lid and transfer to the oven.

Cook for around 45 minutes, or until the lentils are softened, adding more water if it starts to dry out.

Pappardelle with game ragù

I keep a running mental roster of my ten favourite meals ever, and this is among them. A good few years ago I was visiting an old friend who was living in Italy and he took us for a beautiful Saturday walk in the hills above Verona. As with most good walks, we got a little bit lost and finally arrived, tired and hungry, at a small village restaurant at a dangerously late hour. We feared we might be met with the not-uncommon *chiuso* ('closed') mid-afternoon response to our lunch enquiry. But we were lucky and instead sat down to a hearty plate of rabbit ragù with pappardelle, washed down with a bottle of Chianti or two and finished off with a fiery grappa.

Rabbit is not the easiest meat to get hold of in the UK, so you can also use venison or wild boar; both work pretty well for the light gamey flavour that make this such a great dish. Farm shops, farmers' markets and online suppliers (such as pipersfarm.com and blackface.co.uk) are places to source the meat, or a good local butcher where you can ask them to mince the meat for you.

Feeds 4–6, depending on appetite

Preparation time: 15 minutes

Cooking time: 1 hour 10 minutes

40ml (about 3 tablespoons) olive oil

50g (1¾oz) butter

100g (3½oz) finely diced pancetta, or bacon lardons

1 onion, finely chopped

1 carrot, finely chopped

1 celery stick, finely chopped

2 garlic cloves, finely chopped

500g (1lb 2oz) rabbit (1 decent-sized rabbit), or the same weight of venison or wild boar, minced or finely chopped

rosemary sprig

3 sage leaves

⅓ bottle (250ml / 9fl oz) inexpensive white wine

500ml (18fl oz) vegetable stock, or chicken stock

50g (1¾oz) tomato passata

500g (1lb 2oz) pappardelle

sea salt flakes and freshly coarse-ground black pepper

finely grated Parmesan, to serve

Heat the oil and butter in a large frying pan, add the pancetta or bacon and cook over a medium heat for a couple of minutes, stirring occasionally, then add the onion, carrot, celery and garlic to make a good soffritto base. Cook over a medium-low heat for around 5 minutes, until all the vegetables have softened a little.

Next add the meat and cook over a medium-high heat, stirring frequently, until it has started to brown.

Now add the herbs, wine, stock and passata and cook over a low heat for about 1 hour, stirring occasionally, until you have a nice rich ragù. Season with salt and pepper.

Cook your pasta in a large pan of salted boiling water according to the packet instructions, then drain, reserving a small cup of pasta water. Return the pasta to the pan. Add the ragù and stir well into the pasta, adding a little of your reserved pasta cooking water to loosen the sauce; somehow this always improves it. Serve with a generous grating of Parmesan.

Venison polpette with parmesan polenta

Venison is delicious, healthy and increasingly abundant, whether farmed or as the natural byproduct of the necessity of keeping the UK's deer population at a controlled level, since there are no natural predators. You will find farmed venison in most supermarkets, but there are also several online sellers that are worth checking out for wild venison (such as blackface.co.uk and fieldandflower.co.uk). We eat quite a lot of venison at home. Where we spend our holidays, there is a large native Sika deer population and the venison from these deer, originally from Japan, is considered by many chefs to be the tastiest of all, but I am keen on all types.

Venison makes delicious burgers, ideally mixed with a little minced pork as it is a little too lean on its own, and a deboned leg of venison for the barbecue is a good alternative to lamb cooked the same way. One of my favourite ways to eat venison is made into Italian meatballs: minced venison mixed with pork to add succulence and a generous handful of Parmesan for that quintessential Italian flavour. Served with a classic tomato sauce and accompanied by Parmesan polenta, they are top notch!

Feeds 4

Preparation time: 20 minutes

Cooking time: 45 minutes

For the tomato sauce

10g (¼oz) butter

1 tablespoon olive oil

1 large onion, finely chopped

1 celery stick, finely chopped

1 small carrot, finely chopped

1 large garlic clove, finely chopped

500g (1lb 2oz) tomato passata

pinch of sugar

splash of red wine (optional)

sea salt flakes and freshly ground black pepper

For the meatballs

300g (10½oz) minced venison

150g (5½oz) minced pork
(I'd go for a higher fat content, if there's a choice)

1 garlic clove, crushed

100g (3½oz) fresh white breadcrumbs

30ml (1fl oz / 2 tablespoons) milk

40g (1½oz) Parmesan, finely grated, plus more to serve

2 tablespoons olive oil

8 medium sage leaves, or large leaves cut in half, or shredded basil leaves

For the polenta

1 litre (1¾ pints) milk

200ml (7fl oz) double cream

200g (7oz) polenta, or cornmeal

100g (3½oz) Parmesan, finely grated

50g (1¾oz) butter

sea salt flakes and freshly ground black pepper

continued overleaf

Start by making your classic tomato sauce. Heat the butter and oil together in a deep frying pan or sauté pan and then add the onion, celery, carrot and garlic to the pan. Season with salt and pepper, then cook over a low heat for about 15 minutes, stirring every now and then to ensure nothing burns. Add the passata, a small pinch of sugar (and a splash of wine if you have it to hand) and continue to cook over a low heat for another 15 minutes, stirring occasionally. Taste and adjust the seasoning.

Meanwhile, make the meatballs. Combine all the ingredients except the oil and sage in a mixing bowl and mix them together thoroughly with your hands. Form the mixture into ping-pong-sized balls, rolling them between your hands and putting them on a large plate as you make them.

Heat the 2 tablespoons oil in a frying pan. If you are using the sage, fry the leaves over a medium-high heat for a couple of minutes to crisp them up. Set aside on a plate lined with kitchen paper, to absorb the oil. Put the meatballs in the pan and cook over a medium-high heat for about 5 minutes, turning them over to brown the top and bottom.

Put the meatballs into the tomato sauce, adding a splash of just-boiled water if you need to loosen the sauce, and simmer, with a lid half on. They will take around 10 minutes to cook (cut one open to check).

For the polenta, bring the milk and cream just up to boiling point in a heavy-based saucepan and then slowly sprinkle in the polenta. I find mixing it in with a whisk works best. The polenta almost immediately thickens and you need to stir constantly to stop it burning on the bottom as it cooks: a rubber spatula is best here. Fine/instant polenta or cornmeal cooks in about 3 minutes; more coarse-grained takes about 15 minutes.

To finish off your polenta, stir in your grated Parmesan and butter, season well and cook briefly, stirring, until the cheese and butter have melted.

Serve the meatballs and sauce with the polenta and the sage leaves crumbled over, if using, or scatter with shredded basil leaves, with a final grating of Parmesan.

Charlie's tip Any leftover polenta can be poured into a lightly oiled tin and left to set. Keep in the fridge, covered, then cut into rectangles to fry for another meal.

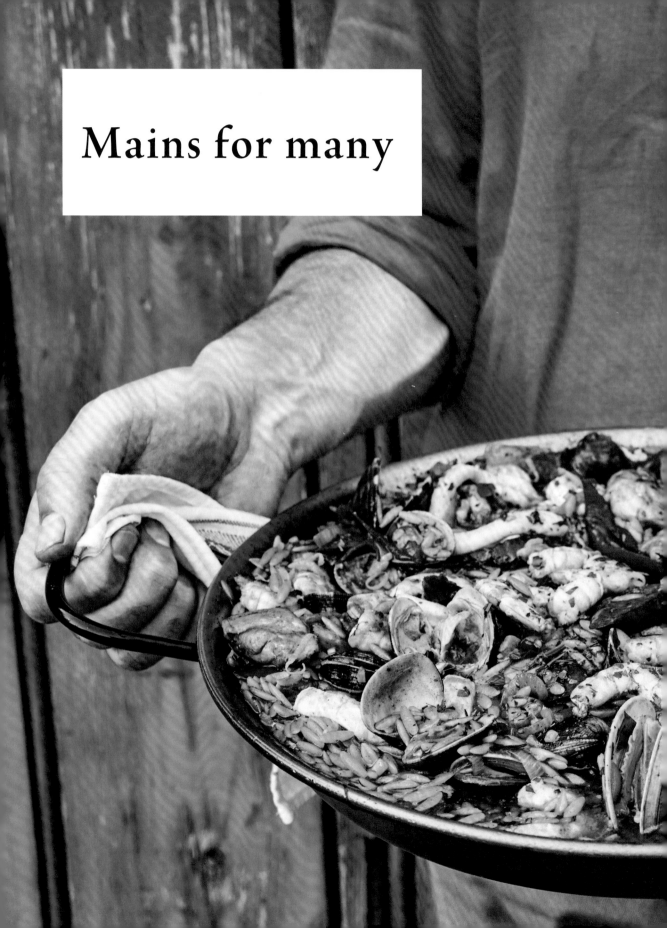

Mains for many

Moules marinière

Mussels are a bountiful, affordable ingredient and we are lucky to have very good ones on the UK coast. If you live somewhere near the sea, you may be able to harvest some yourself (take care to get them from clean waters), or if you are near where they are farmed, you can pick up a large bag for a song. Mussels are sold in supermarkets and fishmongers and there are some fantastic online businesses that will send you a fresh bag or two through the post (my favourite is thewrightbrothers.co.uk). Moules marinière is the classic recipe and I think you always get the best results making it at home, as you can be generous with the extra, indulgent ingredients that restaurants usually leave out and that make mussels even more delicious – and I like to use saffron, too!

Feeds 8

Preparation time: 20 minutes

Cooking time: 10 minutes

4kg (9lb) fresh, live mussels

150g (5½oz) butter

6 large banana shallots, finely chopped

6 large garlic cloves, finely chopped

500ml (18fl oz) inexpensive white wine

400ml (14fl oz) double cream

generous pinch of saffron threads

leaves from 2 large bunches of flat leaf parsley (about 100g / 3½oz), chopped

sea salt flakes and freshly ground black pepper

fresh crusty bread, to serve

It's worth giving the mussels a quick clean first. If you've bought farmed mussels this will involve little more than a quick rinse under cold water and possibly pulling off a few 'beards'. If you've been in hunter-gatherer mode then you will need to wash them more thoroughly, including scraping a few barnacles off the shells using a blunt knife. Discard any that are cracked, don't close when you tap them on the work surface, or don't open when cooked.

I use a huge pan, but alternatively it is best to cook the mussels in 2 large saucepans or wide-based casseroles, to ensure they cook evenly. Over a medium heat, melt half the butter in each pan, then add half the shallots and garlic to each. Cook over a medium heat for 3 minutes, until softened, stirring regularly.

Add the white wine, cream and saffron – half each into the 2 pans. Season with a pinch of salt and lots of pepper. Bring to a gentle simmer and cook for a couple of minutes, stirring until the saffron softens and begins to colour the liquid.

Tip the mussels into the pans, cover and continue to cook over a medium heat for 5 minutes, giving a proper stir every couple of minutes: it's important to move the mussels from the top to the bottom of the pan. You will see those on the bottom opening up to reveal their luscious, orange insides.

At the last minute, stir in the chopped parsley, then serve in warmed bowls. Best accompanied by some lovely fresh bread to mop up all those delicious juices.

Orzo paella

Paella is a real treat when made well. Some people get a bit wound up by what constitutes a 'proper' paella; the inclusion of chorizo is anathema to most Spaniards (but I think is pretty tasty), while others have strong opinions on which seafood should or shouldn't be in there. I've eaten many over the years and they are never quite the same. Among the most enjoyable have been a paella made with squid ink to produce a strikingly black, richly flavoured dish, another with the traditional rabbit rather than chicken, and a particularly delicious version in Valencia – the home of paella – with baby clams and huge, just-off-the-boat prawns. So I'm pretty relaxed about my paellas, as I think there is more than one wonderful recipe, and here I'm risking the ire of my Valencian friends by using orzo pasta rather than the traditional rice, partly because it is slightly quicker to cook and needs less stirring.

Feeds 8

Preparation time: 10 minutes

Cooking time: 30 minutes

50g (1¾oz) butter

50ml (3½ tablespoons) olive oil, plus more for the squid

250g (9oz) chorizo, cut into 1–2cm (½–¾ inch) slices

3 onions, sliced

2 red peppers, sliced into strips

6 garlic cloves, finely chopped

4 skinless boneless chicken thighs, each cut into 5–6 pieces

1 teaspoon chilli flakes

2 tablespoons smoked sweet paprika (pimentón dulce)

½ teaspoon saffron threads (optional, but good)

500g (1lb 2oz) orzo

1.5 litres (2½ pints) hot fresh chicken stock

400g (14oz) clams in their shells (optional, but tasty)

400g (14oz) squid rings

400g (14oz) extra-large raw peeled king prawns

leaves from a bunch of flat leaf parsley (about 30g / 1oz), roughly chopped

finely grated zest and juice of 1 lemon

sea salt flakes and freshly ground black pepper

Melt the butter with the oil in a large, deep frying pan, shallow casserole dish or paella pan over a medium heat. Add the chorizo and cook for a minute or so, to let its flavours run into the fat. Stir in the onions, red peppers and garlic, season with salt and pepper and cook for 5 minutes.

Add the chicken and cook for around 10 minutes, stirring from time to time.

Now add the chilli, smoked paprika and saffron, if using. Stir in the orzo so the grains are well coated, then pour in the chicken stock. Bring to the boil, then reduce the heat to a simmer and cook, stirring from time to time to help the dish cook evenly. The orzo should take about 10 minutes to cook. Add the clams halfway through, if using (don't add any that are open or cracked, and discard any that don't open after cooking).

In a separate frying pan, heat a little olive oil and then flash-fry the squid rings, followed by the prawns, seasoning them with salt and pepper. They will only need a few minutes each. Add any liquid from the fried seafood to the paella.

Once the orzo is cooked, check the seasoning, adding more salt and pepper if necessary, then stir in your parsley and lemon juice. Scatter your cooked prawns and squid over the top, scatter over the lemon zest as a final flourish, and you are ready to take the whole dish straight to the table.

Fish pie

We all love a fish pie. It's our top-selling dish at Charlie Bigham's and had to be in this cookbook. Quite a lot of people write to us about it, sometimes with suggestions such as adding prawns, scallops or hard-boiled eggs. Over the years we have tried all these, but have decided to keep our recipe nice and simple: salmon, smoked haddock and hake (a close cousin of cod). If you are making fish pie at home, please do amend the recipe below, switching some of our choice of fish for your own mixture … and even include the hard-boiled egg, if you insist!

Feeds 8–10

Preparation time: 30 minutes

Cooking time: 1½ hours

500g (1lb 2oz) skinless salmon fillet, cut into 4–5cm (2 inch) chunks

600g (1lb 5oz) skinless hake, cod or haddock fillet, cut into 4–5cm (2 inch) chunks

175g (6oz) young spinach, tough stalks removed, or baby spinach

25g (1oz) dried white breadcrumbs

60g (2¼oz) mature Cheddar, finely grated

2–3 heaped tablespoons chopped flat leaf parsley leaves

For the sauce

100g (3½ oz) butter

90g (3¼oz) plain flour

750ml (1¼ pints) milk

250ml (9fl oz) double cream

240g (8½oz) skinless smoked haddock, cut into 4–5cm (2 inch) chunks

juice of 1 lemon

sea salt flakes and freshly ground black pepper

For the mash

1.6kg (3lb 8oz) floury potatoes, preferably Maris Piper, peeled and cut into even-sized chunks

70g (2½oz) butter

125ml (4fl oz) double cream

2 large egg yolks, lightly beaten

Preheat the oven to 200°C/180°C fan (400°F), Gas Mark 6.

Put the salmon and hake into a large (3 litre / 5¼ pint) ovenproof dish, spreading the chunks out into a single layer. Bake for just 8 minutes – you don't want the fish to fully cook, but you do want to drive off some of its liquid. Set aside.

Meanwhile, put the spinach in a large saucepan with 3 tablespoons of water. Cover and cook over a medium heat for 5 minutes, or until wilted, stirring halfway. Drain in a colander and squeeze out the water. Set aside.

To make the sauce, melt the butter in a large saucepan over a medium heat. Stir in the flour and slowly add the milk, stirring constantly until smooth. Then add the cream, smoked haddock, lemon juice and black pepper. Tip in the fishy cooking juices from your resting salmon and hake (it's extra flavour too good to waste). Simmer very gently over a low heat for 15 minutes, stirring regularly and allowing the smoked haddock to really infuse the sauce. Season with salt and pepper if needed.

Stir the cooked spinach into the sauce, then gently fold in the cooked fish, to ensure you retain big chunks. Tip the whole lot into the ovenproof dish and, ideally, allow to cool (this makes it easier to create a defined layer between the fish and the mash).

For the mash, boil or steam the potatoes, then drain and mash, adding first the butter, then the cream and finally the egg yolks, which will give your mash a lovely colour and extra richness.

Preheat the oven to 200°C/180°C fan (400°F), Gas Mark 6 once more, if you turned it off while the fish filling was cooling.

Spread the mash over the fish filling and finish by sprinkling the top of your pie with the breadcrumbs, grated Cheddar and chopped parsley. Cook in the oven for about 30 minutes, or until the sauce is piping hot and the top is golden, allowing a bit more cooking time if the pie was cold when it went into the oven.

Boneless whole chickens with two marinades

A boneless chicken is easy to marinate, cook and serve, as well as perfect for cooking on the barbecue if the sun comes out. In our company kitchens we debone a lot of chickens. An expert team of butchers, armed with razor-sharp knives, can do the job in 40 seconds with just a few deft cuts. My capability is a little more modest, but I can now make a passable effort in about five minutes and you can take a peek at me deploying my amateur skills at www.charliebighams.com/cookbook. Practice makes perfect, so don't worry if your chicken looks a bit of a mess the first couple of times you do it; it's easier with as large a chicken as possible. A butcher will also debone your chicken, given notice. Or you can use chicken thighs instead (see tip on page 131). The other great thing about a boneless chicken is that you can alter the number of people it serves by the size of bird you choose. A 1.2kg (2lb 12oz) chicken serves three or four people, a 2kg (4lb 8oz) bird will comfortably serve six, while the sort of large chicken you might find in a farm shop (closer to 3kg / 6lb 8oz) can stretch to ten. I've based the marinade quantities below on a 2kg chicken, so you may need to adjust those up or down a bit for a bigger or smaller bird.

When it comes to marinades, the world is your oyster. Have fun experimenting with flavours you like. Here I'm giving you two alternatives for inspiration. The maple syrup and soy sauce version with rosemary and garlic is from my good friend Andy, who is never happier than when standing over smouldering coals, so I recommend this for the barbecue. My Mediterranean marinade is great all year round for supper or a Sunday lunch. Both marinades work well with a simple Salsa Verde, so I've included that recipe in this book for good measure (see page 181).

Feeds 12 (easy to scale down for 6 or scale up for a bigger crowd)

Preparation time: 15 minutes, plus marinating and resting

Cooking time: 45 minutes in an oven, a little less on a barbecue (depending on temperature)

---

2 x 2kg (4lb 8oz) whole chickens, deboned (ask your butcher to prepare them, or see tip overleaf)

Salsa Verde (see page 181) and Green Salad with Roast Artichokes & Avocado (see page 154), to serve

For the maple, soy, rosemary and garlic marinade (for 1 x 2kg / 4lb 8oz bird)

4 tablespoons extra virgin olive oil, plus 1–2 tablespoons to baste (optional)

3 tablespoons dark soy sauce

2 tablespoons maple syrup

juice of ½ large lemon

2 garlic cloves, crushed

leaves from 10 rosemary sprigs, finely chopped (you'll need 3 tablespoons), plus more branches to serve (optional)

For the Mediterranean marinade (for 1 x 2kg / 4lb 8oz bird)

100g (3½oz) sun-blush (semi-dried) tomatoes, drained

100ml (3½fl oz) extra virgin olive oil, plus 1–2 tablespoons to baste (optional)

finely grated zest and juice of 2 lemons

3 garlic cloves, roughly chopped

leaves from 3 rosemary sprigs, plus more branches to serve (optional)

leaves from ½ bunch of flat leaf parsley (about 15g / ½oz), roughly chopped

sea salt flakes and freshly ground black pepper

continued overleaf

For the maple marinade, combine the ingredients together in a mixing bowl with a generous amount of salt and pepper.

For the Mediterranean marinade, put all the ingredients, plus generous amounts of salt and pepper, in a food processor and blitz until well combined.

For either recipe, put your chicken in a large, non-metallic bowl along with all the marinade. Use your hands to massage the marinade into the chicken, making sure all the surfaces are well covered. Cover and leave to marinate in the fridge for at least 3 hours, but preferably overnight. Allow to return to room temperature before cooking.

When you are ready to cook, transfer your marinated chicken into either a large baking tray or roasting tin and push down to ensure the chicken is flattened, or place straight on to a barbecue with nice hot coals. (If using a barbecue, test the heat by holding the palm of your hand over where you plan to cook the chicken: you should be able to hold it there for 10 seconds or so before it gets too hot.)

You should find there is some marinade left in the bottom of the bowl; if you are cooking on a barbecue, add the 1–2 tablespoons more olive oil to this.

For oven cooking, preheat the oven to 200°C/180°C fan (400°F), Gas Mark 6. Cook the chicken for around 45 minutes (you will need to adjust the cooking time for smaller or larger birds).

For either cooking method I'm a fan of basting halfway through cooking. Take the meat off the barbecue, or out of the oven, and whirl it round in the leftover marinade, before putting back on the grill or in the oven. This way, more of the marinade flavours infuse into the chicken.

Rest the chicken for 5 minutes or so before carving. I like to serve this on a bed of rosemary branches, if you have a rosemary plant at home, with Salsa Verde and a Green Salad with Roast Artichokes & Avocado.

Charlie's tip If you can't face deboning a whole chicken (or that's going to be just too much meat), an alternative is to buy some chicken thighs. The skin is important for both flavour and optimum cooking, so go for the skin-on, bone-in thighs, then just remove the single bone from each thigh. I reckon two thighs per person.

Chicken tikka masala

As we all know, this has become an adopted national dish, but how many of us ever make it at home? This is based on the recipe we use at Charlie Bigham's and is well worth making yourself if you've got lots of people coming round. My two key tips from years of honing our recipe are to marinate the chicken first, and to get the spices right by adding them at the correct stage of cooking.

Feeds 9–10

Preparation time: 30 minutes, plus marinating

Cooking time: 1 hour

For the chicken

1.25kg (2lb 12oz) skinless boneless chicken breast or thighs

150g (5½oz) full-fat natural yogurt

3 garlic cloves, finely grated

30g (1oz) root ginger, finely grated

2 teaspoons ground cumin

2 teaspoons ground coriander

½ teaspoon cayenne pepper

1 teaspoon sea salt flakes

scant ½ teaspoon ground turmeric

2 teaspoons garam masala

a little oil, for the tray

freshly ground black pepper

For the sauce

100g (3½oz) butter

3 onions, finely sliced

½–2 teaspoons cayenne pepper, to taste

2 red chillies, deseeded and chopped (or more/less to taste)

2 teaspoons ground coriander

2 teaspoons ground fenugreek

4 teaspoons ground ginger

8 garlic cloves, finely grated

100g (3½oz) tomato purée

80g (2¾oz) mango chutney

20g (¾oz) lime pickle

400ml (14fl oz) double cream

250ml (9fl oz) milk

2 teaspoons garam masala

First, marinate your chicken. Cut up the chicken into bite-sized pieces and mix thoroughly with all the other ingredients for the chicken in a large mixing bowl. Cover and leave in the fridge for a few hours, or ideally overnight.

Make your sauce. Melt the butter in a large saucepan and sweat your onions over a medium-low heat until they become translucent, stirring occasionally (about 10 minutes).

Add the cayenne, chillies, coriander, fenugreek, ginger and garlic. Cook over a low heat for a further 10 minutes, stirring regularly.

Stir in the tomato purée, mango chutney and lime pickle, then add the double cream and milk. Warm the sauce over a medium heat for 6–8 minutes, stirring quite often and not allowing it to come to the boil.

Blend the sauce with a stick blender until smooth; this might take 5 minutes.

Turn the oven to its hottest setting and lightly oil a large baking tray. Place half the chicken pieces on the tray in a single layer and bake for 10 minutes until lightly toasted in places. Set the cooked chicken on a plate and repeat with the remaining chicken. (You can do this in a single batch if you have 2 large baking trays.)

Tip your chicken, and any resting juices, into the sauce and simmer the curry over a low heat for around 10 minutes, stirring regularly or until the chicken is cooked through, adding the garam masala at the end.

Charlie's tip You can make the sauce in advance and reheat it as the marinated chicken is cooking.

Beef topside for picnics

This might seem an odd 'recipe' … and indeed it is, being not so much a detailed list of ingredients as a good idea for a near-perfect picnic lunch. The idea came about one summer when a bunch of us went off on a boating expedition in a hurry. We needed a picnic, there wasn't much food knocking about and nobody had time to go shopping. Fortunately, I stumbled across a rolled topside of beef sitting in the fridge, so into the oven it went. Some crusty bread, a few green leaves, a smear of Dijon mustard or horseradish (maybe both) and you will find yourself enjoying the ultimate gourmet picnic sandwich.

Feeds 12

Preparation time: 5 minutes, plus resting

Cooking time: 55 minutes

1.5kg (3lb 5oz) rolled topside of beef

4 baguettes, or a dozen crusty rolls

jar of horseradish sauce

jar of Dijon mustard

fresh leaves – rocket or lamb's lettuce are ideal, but whatever is to hand

Preheat the oven to 180°C/160°C fan (350°F), Gas Mark 4.

Chuck the topside into the hot oven in a large roasting tin, leaving it in its netting or string and cooking with the fat side on top. Cook for 55 minutes (or until it reaches 55°C / 131°F if using a meat thermometer) for lovely pink beef, longer if you insist and are happy with brown meat.

Once cooked, wrap the hot beef as tightly as you can in about 3 layers of foil, then a layer of clingfilm (it might 'bleed' a little) and finally a tea towel. Wrapped like this, your beef will continue cooking a little as it rests and will stay warm for at least 2 hours.

Be sure to taking a decent chopping board and carving knife and fork in your picnic bag.

When the moment arrives to eat, thinly slice the warm beef and enjoy in a crusty baguette or roll with a healthy dollop of horseradish and/or Dijon mustard and some good fresh leaves.

The ultimate lasagne

Lasagne was the first recipe I ever made. My mum is a lasagne supremo and gave me my first lesson at the age of 12; I have been making it ever since. At Charlie Bigham's, we've spent a long time refining our recipe to ensure it's second to none – and we keep tweaking it to make it even better. This dish is based on that recipe, but I've made a few tweaks to speed things up a bit. The secret to a great – rather than an average – lasagne is twofold: a carefully constructed, slow-cooked ragù and multiple layers. For the ragù, it's important to brown the meat first before it goes into the sauce to be slow-cooked. Within the sauce itself are some special ingredients that make a real difference: white wine rather than red (as called for in the original Italian recipe); three sorts of tomato (chopped canned, passata and purée); a very small amount of chicken liver for depth; and the subtle flavour notes of nutmeg, oregano, star anise and balsamic vinegar. When it comes to the layering stage, choose a large, deep ovenproof dish so you can have multiple layers of pasta: I recommend at least five.

Feeds 10

Preparation time: 30 minutes

Cooking time: 1¾–2 hours

---

about 10 sheets of fresh lasagne, or 20 sheets of dried lasagne (see tip, overleaf)

30g (1oz) Parmesan, finely grated

30g (1oz) mature Cheddar, finely grated

2 heaped tablespoons chopped parsley leaves, or basil leaves

For the béchamel

50g (1¾oz) butter

50g (1¾oz) plain flour

600ml (20fl oz) full-fat milk

pinch of ground nutmeg

150g (5½oz) mature Cheddar, finely grated

100ml (3½fl oz) double cream

sea salt flakes

For the ragù

20g (¾oz) butter

2 tablespoons olive oil

2 onions, finely chopped

2 carrots, finely chopped

2 celery sticks, finely chopped

500g (1lb 2oz) minced beef, at least 12 per cent fat

500g (1lb 2oz) minced pork

200g (7oz) bacon lardons

3 garlic cloves, finely chopped

50g (1¾oz) chicken livers, trimmed and chopped (optional, but worth it!)

¼ teaspoon ground star anise

¼ teaspoon freshly ground nutmeg

2 teaspoons balsamic vinegar

800ml (1½ pints) chicken stock, either fresh or made with 1 stock cube

150g (5½oz) tomato purée

2 x 400g (14oz) cans of chopped tomatoes

200g (7oz) tomato passata

350ml (12fl oz) white wine

leaves from 2 oregano sprigs, finely chopped, or 1 teaspoon dried oregano

freshly ground black pepper

continued overleaf

Start with the ragù. First, put the butter and olive oil in a large heavy-based saucepan or casserole along with the onions, carrots and celery. Cook over a low heat for 10–15 minutes, or until the onions are translucent (you don't want them to brown).

Meanwhile, brown the minced beef, minced pork and bacon lardons in a large frying pan over a high heat. Depending on the size of your frying pan you may want to do this in batches. You only need to cook each batch of meat for about 5 minutes, stirring occasionally, so all the pieces are browned all over. Set aside.

Add the garlic, chicken livers, star anise, nutmeg, balsamic vinegar and 2–3 twists of pepper to the cooked onion and carrots. Stir in well and cook over a medium heat for 2–3 minutes.

Now add the cooked meat and all the other ragù ingredients to the onion and carrots. Increase the heat to high until the sauce is bubbling, stirring frequently to ensure it does not burn. Reduce the heat to low, cover the pan loosely with a lid and simmer for about 1 hour, or until the sauce has thickened. Stir occasionally and more often towards the end of the cooking time. The ragù needs to be saucy enough to soften the lasagne as it cooks, but not too runny either. If the sauce reduces too much, add an extra splash of water.

Meanwhile, make your béchamel. Melt the butter in a saucepan and stir in the flour. Slowly add the milk, stirring all the time to ensure there are no lumps. Then add the nutmeg, pepper, cheese and cream. Keep over a low heat until all the cheese is melted and the sauce is smooth. Season with a little salt.

Once both your ragù and béchamel are cooked, you can layer up the lasagne. Choose a large ovenproof dish (3 litre / 5¼ pint, 6–8cm / 2½–3¼ inch deep). Preheat the oven to 220°C/200°C fan (425°F), Gas Mark 7. Starting with a layer of ragù, alternate with pasta sheets. The secret here is to keep each layer of ragù as thin as you can. At the halfway stage, add a layer of half the béchamel in the middle of the lasagne.

Once all your ragù is finished, put on a final layer of pasta, then top with the rest of your béchamel and sprinkle generously with the Parmesan, Cheddar and parsley or basil. Bake until golden brown and bubbling: about 25 minutes, or 40 minutes if you've made it in advance (see tip). Stand for 5 minutes before serving.

Charlie's tips
- I use fresh pasta for my lasagne, which is widely available, but dried is fine; just add a little more water to the ragù.
- You can make your lasagne the day before and keep it, covered, in the fridge – just cook it for longer (about 40 minutes).

Giant fusilli with luganica sauce

This recipe is inspired by the famous (and delicious) luganica sausage that you will find throughout northern Italy. Rather than send you on a hunt around Italian delis to seek it out, I've used minced pork with a few additions so you can make your own version. Combined with a lovely rich tomato sauce flavoured with lots of rosemary and a good dose of chilli, it's a fantastic alternative to a traditional Bolognese sauce, and can easily be scaled up as a great way of feeding a crowd with minimal effort. The classic pasta to accompany a sauce such as this is spaghetti, but give it a whirl with some giant fusilli.

Feeds 8
Preparation time: 15 minutes
Cooking time: 1 hour 20 minutes

50g (1¾oz) butter

50ml (3½ tablespoons) olive oil

4 red onions, finely chopped

2 celery sticks, finely chopped

4 garlic cloves, finely chopped

600g (1lb 5oz) coarsely minced pork

1 teaspoon chilli flakes, or to taste

leaves from a few rosemary sprigs, finely chopped (about 1 teaspoon)

good grating of nutmeg

pinch of ground cinnamon

3 x 400g (14oz) cans of chopped tomatoes (I recommend the Mutti brand)

3 tablespoons tomato purée

200g (7oz) tomato passata

3 bay leaves

800g–1kg (1lb 12oz–2lb 4oz) giant fusilli (aka fusilli giganti / fusilloni), or other pasta shapes

150ml (¼ pint) single cream

leaves from a bunch of flat leaf parsley (about 30g / 1oz), finely chopped

sea salt flakes and freshly ground black pepper

finely grated Parmesan, to serve

Melt the butter in a large, deep frying pan or shallow casserole dish, add the olive oil and then cook the onions, celery and garlic over a medium heat for around 10 minutes, or until the onions have softened.

Add the minced pork and cook for another 10 minutes.

Add the chilli flakes, rosemary, nutmeg, cinnamon and a good seasoning of salt and pepper and mix in thoroughly with the meat and onions. Now stir in the chopped tomatoes, tomato purée, tomato passata and bay leaves. Reduce the heat and simmer, lid on but just slightly ajar, for 1 hour, stirring occasionally, until you have a nice rich sauce, adding a little water if it becomes too thick.

Cook the pasta in a very large saucepan of salted boiling water according to the packet instructions, until al dente, then drain.

To finish your sauce, add the cream and stir. Then combine the pasta and sauce in one pan and mix together well.

Serve with a sprinkling of parsley and lashings of grated Parmesan.

Charlie's tip When working out how much pasta you will need here, figure on about 100g (3½oz) for each person, or more for bigger appetites.

Leg of lamb with harissa & chermoula

I am not a huge fan of a traditional Sunday roast leg of lamb, but I do love lamb. The leg is a great cut to eat, especially when deboned. This is a quick and pretty easy thing to do, given a bit of practice (see tip, overleaf), or you can get a butcher to do it for you. Lamb is the meat of choice in most Middle Eastern countries, so I have gone for some big Middle Eastern flavours here: a spicy harissa to flavour the meat before and during cooking, then a lovely, tasty chermoula to serve with it. When we eat this at home, it's usually as the centrepiece to a Middle Eastern banquet of at least six different dishes. If you want a real feast – and fancy a cookathon – I'd suggest my Tomato, Roasted Pepper & Pomegranate Salad; Couscous with Apricots, Parsley & Red Onion; Chargrilled Courgettes with Feta; Tzatziki; and Roast Aubergines with Garlic & Herbs (see pages 150, 167, 177, 180 and 188). I find an average-sized leg of lamb will comfortably feed ten people when served with other dishes like this, or can even easily stretch to 14 if required. What at first glance can look like a pretty expensive meal can turn out to be good value for money.

Feeds 10–14, with other dishes (see recipe introduction)

Preparation time: 30 minutes, plus marinating (optional) and resting

Cooking time: 1 hour 10 minutes

---

1 whole leg of lamb, about 2.5kg (5lb 8oz), deboned by your butcher or do it yourself (see tip overleaf)

For the harissa (or see tip, overleaf)

2 large red peppers, deseeded and roughly chopped

1 small onion, sliced

6 garlic cloves

4–5 red chillies, destalked (I leave the seeds in)

5 teaspoons cumin seeds

5 teaspoons coriander seeds

70ml (2½fl oz / 4½ tablespoons) extra virgin olive oil

1 tablespoon tomato purée

finely grated zest and juice of 1 lemon

1 teaspoon sea salt flakes

For the chermoula

175ml (6fl oz) extra virgin olive oil

150g (5½oz) fresh coriander

50g (1¾oz) flat leaf parsley

4 garlic cloves

1 preserved lemon, seeds removed (Belazu is my preferred brand)

1 teaspoon sea salt flakes

½ teaspoon paprika

½ teaspoon ground cumin

generous pinch of cayenne pepper

freshly ground black pepper

continued overleaf

Preheat the oven to 200°C/180°C fan (400°F), Gas Mark 6.

First off, make your harissa. Put the peppers, onion, garlic and chillies in a large baking tray. Sprinkle over the cumin seeds and coriander seeds, drizzle the whole lot with half the olive oil and put in the oven for around 25 minutes, or until softened and lightly toasted in places.

Once cooked, tip the whole lot into a food processor or blender and blend to a rough paste with the rest of your olive oil, the tomato purée, lemon zest and juice and salt. Allow to cool a little. Meanwhile flatten your deboned lamb.

If you plan to cook in the oven, take your slightly cooled harissa and spread liberally all over the lamb, working it into the flesh as much as you can. If you plan on barbecuing the meat, rub in only half the harissa. At this point, you can put the lamb into the fridge to cook the following day (allow it to come to room temperature before cooking), or you can cook straight away.

To cook in the oven, preheat the oven to 200°C/180°C fan (400°F), Gas Mark 6. Place the lamb in a large roasting tin and cook for around 45 minutes for pink (or until a meat thermometer shows it is 52°C / 126°F), longer if you prefer medium or well-done meat. The harissa should look lightly coloured and charred in places. Rest the lamb for 15–20 minutes before serving.

If the weather is kind, my preference is to the cook the lamb on a barbecue. Coat all sides of the lamb in the remaining half of the harissa 15 minutes before the end of the cooking time. The time it takes will vary, depending on the heat of your barbecue. I find 45 minutes is generally about right for nice pink lamb, with regular turning, or 52°C (126°F) if you use a probe thermometer.

While the lamb is cooking, you can make your chermoula. Put half the olive oil and all the other ingredients into your food processor or blender and blend until you have a luscious bright green paste, still retaining some texture. Add the remaining oil and blitz again. Season with pepper.

Carve the lamb and serve with the chermoula and side dishes (see recipe introduction).

Charlie's tips
- You can get a butcher to debone your lamb, or do it yourself. Take it slowly the first time and use a sharp knife. To see me having a go, take a peek at www.charliebighams.com/cookbook.
- If you don't want to make your own harissa, there are a few good versions out there, my favourite being Belazu's rose harissa.

Slow-cooked shoulder of lamb with marmite

OK, I know this sounds odd, so you are going to have to trust me! I can't remember where the idea for using Marmite came from, but I've been cooking this for at least 20 years and it goes down well with everyone, even those who don't like Marmite. It's a great way to slow-cook a shoulder of lamb and will leave you with a wonderful pile of 'pulled' meat, which makes a delicious and inexpensive core to a feast. I suggest you serve it with wraps, or – better still – Middle Eastern flatbreads, if you can find some. You will also need some other dishes alongside, I suggest my Orzo with Cherry Tomatoes & Dates; Tzatziki; and Fennel with Honey & Pine Nuts (see pages 159, 180 and 187).

Feeds 8–12 (I like to have less meat and plenty of accompaniments)

Preparation time: 10 minutes

Cooking time: 8¼–24 hours

1.6–2kg (3lb 8oz–4lb 8oz) whole shoulder of lamb

1 small (125g / 4½oz) jar of Marmite

To serve

wraps, or Middle Eastern flatbreads

selection of salads, to serve (see introduction)

Preheat the oven to 200°C/180°C fan (400°F), Gas Mark 6.

Use your hands to smear the lamb with the whole jar of Marmite, making sure the whole surface of the lamb gets a good coating. This is fun, if a little messy! You now need to wrap your lamb as tightly as you can in 3 layers of foil, ensuring there are no gaps.

Place the wrapped lamb in a large roasting tin and tightly wrap the tin in 2 more layers of foil. Put in the oven for about 15 minutes.

Now reduce the oven temperature to 120°C/100°C fan (250°F), Gas Mark ½ and continue cooking the lamb for at least 8 hours; more like 9–10 if using a larger shoulder. If you have an Aga, you can put the lamb into the coldest oven and cook it for up to 24 hours.

Once your lamb is cooked, remove it from the oven, reserve about half the cooking juices and pour away the rest (you'll find there are a lot and they are salty) and unwrap it from its foil layers. The meat will have fallen off the bones, so you should be able to pick out the large bones and throw them away.

Now shred the lamb (2 large forks works well for this), pour over some of the cooking juices and serve warm, with wraps and a selection of salads.

Vegetable sides & sharing plates

Tomato, roasted pepper & pomegranate salad

Colourful food is good food, and this gorgeous red salad gives any spread an adrenaline shot of colour. I've used a mix of cherry tomatoes and some wonderful heritage varieties, but you can use whatever tomatoes you like – just try and find some that are ripe and full of flavour. For the peppers, I tend to use Romano, while for the pomegranate it's worth the effort to buy a whole fruit and prepare it yourself rather than going for a plastic tub.

Feeds 6

Preparation time: 5 minutes

Cooking time: 25 minutes

400g (14oz) Romano red peppers, halved, deseeded and chopped

olive oil

400g (14oz) tomatoes

seeds from 1 pomegranate

extra virgin olive oil

pomegranate molasses

a few thyme sprigs

sea salt flakes

Preheat the oven to 200°C/180°C fan (400°F), Gas Mark 6.

Put the red peppers in a large roasting tin, drizzle generously with regular olive oil and sprinkle with a little salt. Roast for 20–25 minutes, or until cooked through and starting to brown. Leave to cool.

Meanwhile, slice up the tomatoes.

Once the red peppers are cooked, mix with the tomatoes and pomegranate seeds and put on a large, flat serving dish. Drizzle over some extra virgin olive oil and pomegranate molasses and sprinkle with a few thyme sprigs.

Carrots with pumpkin seeds & a sesame dressing

In my view, raw carrots are generally nicer than cooked carrots, especially if you seek out those grown in a non-intensive way (keep an eye out in farm shops for carrots still with their green tops on). Mix in some grated red cabbage and you have this lovely colourful dish with a tasty dressing.

Feeds 6

Preparation time: 5 minutes

500g (1lb 2oz) carrots, topped, peeled if you want, but you might lose some of those good healthy nutrients

300g (10½oz) red cabbage, outer leaves trimmed

50g (1¾oz) pumpkin seeds

60ml (2¼fl oz / 4 tablespoons) toasted sesame oil

juice of 1–2 limes (about 2 tablespoons)

20ml (¾fl oz / 4 teaspoons) soy sauce

4 teaspoons runny honey

sea salt flakes and freshly ground black pepper

Coarsely grate the carrots and red cabbage.

Toast the pumpkin seeds in a hot, dry frying pan for a few seconds. Watch out, as they might pop a bit and start jumping out of the pan. Tip out on to a plate.

Make the dressing: put the sesame oil, lime juice, soy sauce and honey in a mixing bowl and whisk together. Season to taste with salt and pepper.

Add the grated carrot and cabbage to the bowl and mix well to ensure everything is well dressed.

Stir two-thirds of the seeds through the salad and sprinkle the rest on top.

Charlie's tip Only dress the salad just before serving, otherwise lots of liquid comes out of the veg.

Green salad with roast artichokes & avocado

I like to have a green salad on the table at almost every meal. Of course, it's seldom ever the same, since it is largely driven by what I find in the fridge or, in the summer months, what is growing in the garden. As well as a nice mixture of leaves, you can lift a salad by adding a couple of heftier ingredients (here avocados and artichoke hearts), taking a few minutes to make a really great dressing and finishing things off with some croutons, should you have some past-its-peak good bread around. Chargrilled artichoke hearts in oil can often be found in the deli section of the supermarket.

Feeds 6

Preparation time: 10 minutes

Cooking time: 5 minutes

250g (9oz) slightly stale bread, cut into cubes

2 garlic cloves, finely chopped

olive oil

400g (14oz) mixed salad leaves (rocket, oak leaf lettuce, Romaine, red chicory)

200g (7oz) chargrilled artichoke hearts in sunflower oil

2 ripe avocados, pitted, scooped out of their skins and cut into chunks

handful of nasturtium flowers, to serve

For the dressing

1 teaspoon Dijon mustard

1 teaspoon sherry vinegar

100ml (3½fl oz) extra virgin olive oil, or oil from the artichoke jar

juice of ¼ lemon

sea salt flakes and freshly ground black pepper

First, make your croutons; you can do this a couple of hours in advance and keep them in an airtight container until needed. In a frying pan, fry your cubes of bread with the garlic in olive oil until nicely browned. Set aside on a plate lined with kitchen paper, to blot any excess oil.

Wash and prepare your leaves and then spin them dry in a salad spinner. Drain the oil from the artichokes (you can use this for the dressing instead of olive oil) and slice them up.

Make your dressing by putting all the ingredients in a jar and shaking hard. Taste and adjust the seasoning if needed.

Just before you want to eat, combine all the ingredients, except the croutons and nasturtiums, in a salad bowl, give your dressing a quick shake, pour over as much as you want and toss everything together gently. Top off with the croutons and nasturtium flowers just before serving.

Charlie's tip Nasturtiums grow like weeds, so plant a few seeds in the early spring and they will take off and provide you with flowers and peppery leaves for salads. A window-box is all you need.

Cucumber with a zingy dressing

Rupert, our fantastic Head of Food at Charlie Bigham's, introduced me to this lovely fresh summer salad recipe. Cucumbers are a quintessential summer vegetable to me and I love growing them at home in our greenhouse. They are straightforward to produce, look magnificent and taste wonderful.

Feeds 4–6

Preparation time: 10 minutes

For the salad

1 large cucumber, about 525g (1lb 3oz), or 2 small cucumbers, halved and cut into 1–2cm (½ inch) pieces

2 small red onions, finely sliced

4 heaped tablespoons finely shredded mint leaves

4 tablespoons roasted peanuts, roughly chopped

For the dressing

juice of 1½ limes (about 3 tablespoons)

2 garlic cloves, crushed

1 tablespoon fish sauce (nam pla)

1 tablespoon palm sugar, or any brown sugar will suffice

4 tablespoons groundnut oil

Mix all the dressing ingredients, except the oil, in a mixing bowl and allow the sugar to dissolve. After 5 minutes, whisk in the oil.

In a salad bowl, combine the vegetables and mint. Tip over the dressing just before serving and toss well. Scatter the roasted peanuts over each plate of salad.

Orzo with cherry tomatoes & dates

This is a great summer dish that I use a lot when I'm cooking several different recipes for an indeterminate number of people – something that seems to happen quite frequently in our house over the summer months.

Feeds 8–10

Preparation time: 10 minutes

Cooking time: 10–12 minutes

---

1 vegetable stock cube, or 2 tablespoons vegetable stock powder (I use the Marigold brand)

500g (1lb 2oz) orzo

200g (7oz) chopped pitted dates

200g (7oz) cherry tomatoes, halved or quartered

30g (1oz) capers, drained

leaves from a bunch of flat leaf parsley (about 30g / 1oz), roughly chopped

3 tablespoons extra virgin olive oil

sea salt flakes and freshly ground black pepper

Two-thirds fill a large saucepan with cold water and bring to the boil. Stir in the stock to dissolve, add the orzo, return to the boil and cook for 10–12 minutes, or until the pasta is al dente, stirring regularly.

Drain the cooked orzo in a large sieve and run under cold water until cold (you might need to mix it around in the sieve a bit to ensure it all cools).

Put the orzo, dates, tomatoes, capers, parsley and olive oil into a large mixing bowl and mix together thoroughly. Add salt and pepper to taste, then tip the whole mixture into a nice dish and serve.

Warm puy lentils with vegetables & goats' cheese

Puy lentils are full of flavour, and, as well as being delicious hot in soups and casseroles, they also make a great salad that can be eaten warm or cold. The secret to a good lentil salad is to cook them in a flavoursome stock to bring out all their deliciousness, then combine them with ingredients that add interest and extra flavour. Here I've chosen red onions and baby carrots, then topped off the salad with a little crumbled goats' cheese and a classic dressing.

Feeds 6–8

Preparation time: 5 minutes

Cooking time: 20–25 minutes

---

2 red onions, cut into wedges

16 baby, small or Chantenay carrots, ideally with a little of the greenery left on

olive oil

500g (1lb 2oz) Puy lentils

500ml (18fl oz) vegetable stock, or chicken stock (even better, in my view)

1 litre (1¾ pints) water

100g (3½oz) mature goats' cheese, not too hard, but aged beyond cream cheese consistency is best

leaves from a small bunch (about 20g / ¾oz) flat leaf parsley, roughly chopped

sea salt flakes and freshly ground black pepper

For the dressing

juice of 1 lemon

90ml (6 tablespoons) extra virgin olive oil, plus more to serve

1 tablespoon red wine vinegar

Preheat the oven to 220°C/200°C fan (425°F), Gas Mark 7.

Scatter the onions and carrots in a roasting tin, drizzle with regular olive oil, sprinkle with a little sea salt and roast for 20–25 minutes, or until tender and lightly browned.

Meanwhile, put the lentils in a large saucepan with your stock and measured water, bring to the boil, then reduce the heat and simmer for 20–25 minutes, until the lentils are tender but retain a little bite. Drain and tip into a serving bowl.

Mix your dressing ingredients, seasoning generously to taste, then tip over the lentils and mix well.

Scatter the roasted vegetables over the lentils, crumble over the goats' cheese, sprinkle with parsley and finish off with a swirl or so of extra virgin olive oil. Serve warm or at room temperature.

Celeriac rémoulade

Celeriac always strikes me as an unloved vegetable, but apart from a rather ugly and slightly intimidating appearance, I can never really understand why, as it's both delicious and versatile. In this book, you'll find a recipe for Roast Celeriac Stacks with Mushrooms & Spinach (see page 66) and it is also delicious raw, never more so than when used to make a classic rémoulade. This is a strong enough dish to make the centrepiece of a light meal with a few extra accompaniments (as served in the photograph here).

Feeds 10 as an accompaniment, 6 as a light main course

Preparation time: 5 minutes if using a food processor, more if cutting the celeriac by hand

---

1 celeriac (about 600g / 1lb 5oz)

For the dressing

juice of 1 lemon

150g (5½oz) mayonnaise

3 teaspoons Dijon mustard

leaves from ½ bunch of flat leaf parsley (about 15g / ½oz), finely chopped

100g (3½oz) cornichons, finely sliced

sea salt flakes and freshly ground black pepper

To serve

charcuterie

gherkins

crusty bread

Mix all the ingredients for the dressing together in a large mixing bowl, seasoning to taste with salt and pepper.

Peel the celeriac and cut into slices about the thickness of a pound coin (3mm / ⅛ inch). Stack up several slices and cut into matchsticks, about 3mm (⅛ inch) thick. (I also often use the large-hole grater on a food processor – it gets a good texture and is very quick.)

Immediately add the cut celeriac to the lemony dressing so it doesn't discolour. Mix thoroughly. Serve with charcuterie, gherkins and crusty bread.

This keeps well in the fridge for a couple of days, but I prefer to serve it at room temperature, so make sure not to serve it chilled.

Persian rice

We eat a lot of rice in our house. This simple method works well if you've got a few people around and want to elevate your rice a notch or two. You can make the dish some time in advance as its timings are relaxed, as long as you are using a heavy-based pan. The magic of cooking rice this way is the delicious buttery base of cooked rice that ends up at the bottom of the pan, known in Iran as the tahdig or 'bottom of the pot'. Delicious with meat dishes, such as my Lamb Koftas, and with Chicken with Ginger, Cumin, Honey & Almonds (see pages 110 and 100).

Feeds 6
Preparation time: 5 minutes
Cooking time: 45–90 minutes

500g (1lb 2oz) white basmati rice

75g (2¾oz) butter

a few saffron threads

30g (1oz) shelled, unsalted pistachio nuts, roughly chopped

40g (1½oz) sultanas

handful of flat leaf parsley leaves, chopped

sea salt flakes

Two-thirds fill a large heavy-based saucepan – that has a tight-fitting lid – with cold water, add the rice and a pinch of salt and set over a medium heat. Bring to the boil, then remove the rice from the heat and drain using a large sieve.

Rinse out the pan and return to a low heat. Add the butter, and once it has melted add the saffron, then tip in your semi-cooked rice, without stirring. Cover the pan with a tight-fitting lid wrapped in a clean tea towel. If using a gas hob, you can tie a knot in the top of the tea towel to keep it away from the flames.

Reduce the heat to as low as it can go, then leave the rice to cook. If the heat is low enough and you are using a heavy-based pan, you can safely leave the rice cooking for 45 minutes to 1½ hours without it burning.

When you are ready to serve, tip the pan upside down on to a large, flat serving dish (so that the cooked buttery rice is on the top), then sprinkle with your pistachio nuts and sultanas (you may choose to warm those in a small frying pan first). Scatter over the parsley and serve.

Sautéed potatoes with paprika & rosemary

Most people love chips, but I'm not sure they are great when made at home – you really need a deep-fat fryer (I don't have one and don't want one) and a lot of oil. My chip alternative is to fry small squares of potato, either simply with a few rosemary sprigs, some garlic and salt, or I'll use this recipe if I want to go a little further. Delicious with my Bashed Chicken with Parmesan Breadcrumbs; Apple & Walnut Chicken Olives, or Breton Chicken with a Chive Mornay Sauce (see pages 93, 94 and 96).

Feeds 4–6

Preparation time: 10 minutes

Cooking time: 20 minutes

1kg (2lb 4oz) potatoes (no need to be fussy about variety), peeled and cut into roughly 2cm (¾ inch) chunks

25g (1oz) polenta, or cornmeal

½ teaspoon sweet smoked paprika

5 tablespoons olive oil

6 garlic cloves, finely chopped

1 heaped tablespoon finely chopped rosemary leaves

sea salt flakes and freshly ground black pepper

Put the potatoes in a medium-large saucepan and cover with cold water. Bring to the boil over a high heat and cook for 1 minute. Drain in a colander and leave to stand for 5 minutes.

Mix the polenta and paprika in a large bowl with salt and pepper. Add the potatoes and toss together.

Heat the oil in a large frying pan and cook the potatoes over a fairly high heat for 8–10 minutes until tender, or until lightly browned and crisp, starting to turn them after 3–4 minutes.

Reduce the heat and stir in the garlic and rosemary. Toss together for 1–2 minutes more, then taste and season with salt and pepper if needed.

Couscous with apricots, parsley & red onion

A summer salad is useful for serving as part of a general feast. This one works well with almost any grilled or barbecued meat and is also good for soaking up a bit of surplus sauce. You can serve it warm, but generally I prefer it at room temperature. It also makes a fantastic stuffing; I use it to stuff the birds in my Partridge Tagine (see page 106).

Feeds 6–8

Preparation time: 15 minutes

250g (9oz) couscous

350ml (12fl oz) hot vegetable stock (from a stock cube is fine)

4–5 tablespoons extra virgin olive oil

1 red onion, finely chopped

100g (3½oz) dried apricots, ideally unsulphured, cut into small chunks (5mm / ¼ inch is ideal)

finely grated zest and juice of 1 large lemon

leaves from a bunch of flat leaf parsley (about 30g / 1oz), chopped

leaves from a large mint sprig, chopped

100g (3½oz) toasted pine nuts

sea salt flakes and freshly ground black pepper

Tip the couscous into a large heatproof mixing bowl and stir in the stock. Cover with a plate and leave to stand for 10 minutes; all the stock will absorb into the couscous.

Stir the olive oil into the couscous and then add the onion, apricots, lemon zest and juice, parsley, mint and pine nuts. Season with plenty of salt and pepper and mix thoroughly.

Charlie's tip I am the master at burning pine nuts. My tip to avoid this is to start with a hot pan, keep the pine nuts moving and never take your eyes off them. As soon as they are brown, tip them on to a cold plate. Alternatively, delegate the task to someone trustworthy.

Sweet potatoes with red onion & greek yogurt

A nice and simple dish that looks great, this makes a regular appearance if I'm cooking up a feast involving lots of dishes. Surprisingly, the sweet potato is not really a potato at all, merely a distant cousin, and more closely related to the leafy green vegetable morning glory that is used in a lot of East Asian cooking. They are generally considered to be highly nutritious, but that isn't the reason I eat them: I just think they are tasty!

Feeds 6

Preparation time: 10 minutes

Cooking time: 30 minutes

---

4 large sweet potatoes (about 1.2kg / 2lb 12oz)

5 tablespoons olive oil

2 red onions, sliced

3 garlic cloves, finely sliced

150g (5½oz) full-fat Greek yogurt

generous drizzle of pomegranate molasses

big handful of flat leaf parsley leaves, chopped

sea salt flakes and freshly ground black pepper

Preheat the oven to 220°C/200°C fan (425°F), Gas Mark 7.

Peel the sweet potatoes and cut into large chunks, each roughly 2.5–3cm (1 inch). Scatter over a large baking tray or roasting tin, drizzle with 2 tablespoons of the olive oil and toss to coat. Roast for about 30 minutes, or until soft and starting to brown. It's a good idea to give them a toss halfway through cooking, to ensure all sides are cooked.

Meanwhile, tip the red onions into a large, deep frying pan with the remaining 3 tablespoons of oil and cook over a low heat for 15–20 minutes, or until softened and lightly browned, adding the sliced garlic halfway through. Stir often, so they cook evenly.

Arrange the cooked sweet potatoes on a flat serving dish, season with salt and pepper, scatter over the cooked red onions, then spoon over the yogurt, drizzle with the pomegranate molasses and sprinkle with plenty of chopped parsley.

Indulgent dauphinoise potatoes

Cooks can rush this classic potato dish, but just a bit more time and a few extra ingredients make all the difference to a dauphinoise, transforming it from ordinary to extraordinary. There's no holding back here: crème fraîche, two types of cheese, Dijon mustard, a big hit of garlic and herbs all help take this dauphinoise up a notch or two. Perfect with Beef Bourguignon (see page 109).

Feeds 8

Preparation time: 10 minutes

Cooking time: 60 minutes, or about 1 hour 15 minutes if using a deeper dish

---

500ml (18fl oz) double cream

500g (1lb 2oz) crème fraîche

2 teaspoons Dijon mustard

pinch of freshly grated nutmeg

5 garlic cloves, crushed

4 bay leaves

5–6 thyme sprigs

1.8kg (4lb) floury potatoes (about 8 large), such as Maris Piper, peeled (about 1.4kg / 3lb peeled weight)

10g (¼oz) butter, for the dish

100g (3½oz) Gruyère cheese, grated

50g (1¾oz) Parmesan, grated

sea salt flakes and freshly ground black pepper

Preheat the oven to 200°C/180°C fan (400°F), Gas Mark 6.

Combine your cream, crème fraîche, mustard, nutmeg and garlic along with the bay and thyme in a large saucepan and bring to the boil. Simmer for 2 minutes, then remove from the heat.

Slice up your potatoes as finely as you can. I tend to use the food processor fitted with the slicing blade for a speedy and consistent result so the potatoes cook evenly.

Arrange half the sliced potatoes over a buttered 3 litre (5¼ pint) ovenproof dish, seasoning with a good sprinkling of salt and a twist or 3 of pepper. I use a dish about 3cm (1¼ inches) deep, or you could also use a deeper dish, such as you might for a lasagne. Pour over some of your warm cream mix, then scatter with about half the Gruyère. Then add the rest of the potatoes, seasoning with salt as you go, and the rest of the warm cream, before finishing off with the rest of the Gruyère, all the Parmesan and a little more pepper.

Put the dish on a foil-lined baking tray and put in the oven for about 1 hour, or until the potatoes are browning on top and soft all the way through. (The cooking time will be a bit longer if you are using a deep dish.) If the top is starting to look a little too brown, loosely place a piece of foil on the top.

Charlie's tip I suggest putting your oven dish on a baking tray before you put it in the oven, as it makes it much easier to take out and will also catch any overspill if the dauphinoise bubbles over.

Spring onion tortilla

Tortillas are great fun to make, hugely satisfying to eat and a well-made tortilla is a thing of beauty! Delicious hot or cold, any remains can sit happily in the fridge for a couple of days to be nibbled away with great pleasure. I also suggest taking this on a picnic, with my Beef Topside (see page 135).

Feeds 8

Preparation time: 10 minutes

Cooking time: 50 minutes

---

6 onions, thinly sliced

8 tablespoons olive oil

2 bunches of spring onions, roughly chopped

1kg (2lb 4oz) floury potatoes, ideally Maris Piper

9 large eggs

1 red chilli, finely chopped (optional)

sea salt flakes and freshly ground black pepper

Cook the onions in a large, deep frying pan or sauté pan (ideally nonstick) with 3 tablespoons of the olive oil over a low heat for 15–20 minutes, or until they have softened, reduced in volume and are just beginning to brown, stirring regularly. The pan will need a lid that fits it well for when you make the tortilla. Add three-quarters of the spring onions and cook for a further 2 minutes, stirring.

Meanwhile, pour enough water into a large saucepan so it is one-third full, then place over a high heat. Bring to the boil. Peel the potatoes and cut into approximately 2cm (¾ inch) chunks. Carefully add the potatoes to the boiling water and return to a simmer. Cook for 8–10 minutes, or until tender but still holding their shape. Drain well.

Whisk the eggs together lightly in a large mixing bowl. Add the cooked potatoes and onions. Season with plenty of salt, pepper and, if you like, chilli. Mix well.

Pour about 3 tablespoons of olive oil into the cleaned-out deep nonstick frying pan or sauté pan and place over a medium heat. Once hot, tip in your tortilla mix and cover the pan with its lid.

Cook over a low heat (as low as you can) for about 20 minutes. While the tortilla is cooking, remove the lid a couple of times, and, with a palette knife, ease the tortilla away from the edges of the pan (this will make it easier to tip out once cooked). The tortilla should be fairly well cooked, with the egg on top starting to set.

Now the moment has come: the flip! Take the tortilla off the heat, remove the lid and replace with a large, flat plate. Holding a tea towel under the frying pan, flip the whole pan upside down. The tortilla should come out of the pan and on to the plate (if it doesn't straight away, tap the bottom of the frying pan with a wooden spoon).

Give the frying pan a good wipe clean and add 2 tablespoons more olive oil. Once the oil is hot, slide the tortilla back into the pan uncooked-side down, scatter over the reserved spring onions, cover, then cook for a final 8–10 minutes or so, until set.

Repeat the flip on to your (now cleaned) plate and – voilà – a beautiful and delicious tortilla is ready to go. Delicious to take on a picnic, eat warm or put in the fridge to eat cold later.

Romano roast peppers

You may have noticed that I've got a soft spot for red peppers and this simple recipe is a celebration of them. It's delicious served as a vegetable accompaniment, but also makes a good starter or light lunch with some salad and bread. I always prefer the long Romano peppers when I can find them, or you can use regular peppers. The secret is to slow-roast them in plenty of olive oil and add a judicious number of extra ingredients to bring them to life. Here I've used shallots, tomatoes, garlic, capers and thyme. If you want a little bit more flavour oomph, add a good-quality roughly chopped anchovy (either white or canned) to each pepper.

Feeds 6

Preparation time: 10 minutes

Cooking time: 25–30 minutes

---

6 Romano red peppers, halved and deseeded

2 tomatoes, roughly chopped

2 banana shallots, finely chopped

4 large garlic cloves, finely chopped

4 teaspoons capers

leaves from a few sprigs of thyme

5 tablespoons olive oil

sea salt flakes and freshly ground black pepper

Preheat the oven to 200°C/180°C fan (400°F), Gas Mark 6.

Put the prepared peppers into a baking tray cut-side up and scatter the tomatoes, shallots and garlic, capers and thyme over the top, ensuring that each pepper gets its fair share of filling, and season well. Douse the whole dish with the olive oil.

Bake for 25–30 minutes, or until the peppers are soft.

Charlie's tip Five minutes before the end of cooking, I like to scatter some mozzarella over the peppers and put them back in the oven.

Chargrilled courgettes with feta

Courgettes are a wonderful vegetable, easy to grow and delicious to eat. The secret to courgettes in the kitchen is to never put them anywhere near water: a minor food crime. Fry them, griddle them, bake them, barbecue them – just never boil them. The best tool for this recipe is a griddle pan or barbecue, to get the chargrilled stripes and flavour.

Feeds 4

Preparation time: 5 minutes

Cooking time: 20 minutes

3 medium-large courgettes (total weight about 500g / 1lb 2oz), trimmed

4 tablespoons extra virgin olive oil

3 garlic cloves, finely sliced

½ red chilli, finely chopped or sliced, or a large pinch of chilli flakes

100g (3½oz) feta cheese

freshly ground black pepper

Put your griddle pan over a high heat to get it really nice and hot. Once it starts smoking, reduce the heat to medium. Or get the barbecue nice and hot.

Slice the courgettes lengthways, so the slices are about 3mm (⅛ inch) thick: you want them elegantly thin and the thinner they are the quicker they cook. You should end up with about 6 slices for each courgette. Toss the courgettes in 1 tablespoon of the oil until very lightly coated.

In batches, cook the courgettes on the griddle, or over the barbecue. The secret is not to keep picking them up to see if they look done, but put them down once and leave them; this way you end up with elegantly striped courgettes. As soon as you see a hint of smoke coming off the courgettes, it's time to flip them over.

While the courgettes are cooking, put the remaining oil, garlic and chilli in a small frying pan over a low heat and cook for just 1–2 minutes, or until softened but not coloured. Set aside.

Once the courgettes are cooked on both sides, lay them out on a large flat dish, season with pepper, crumble over the feta and douse with the garlic-chilli oil. Delicious served either warm or at room temperature.

Courgette fritters with mint & feta

Simple and delicious, these are a great side dish to have on the table when you have a few people round and a spread of several different dishes, and especially good if you have a vegetarian or two in the party. I like to serve them with a bowl of Tzatziki (see page 180) not too far away. This is a hands-on dish to make, so be prepared to get covered in food and enjoy getting stuck in! Although best served just-cooked, you can make these fritters a little in advance and keep them warm in the oven covered in foil.

Feeds 4 / Makes 12 small fritters

Preparation time: 10 minutes

Cooking time: 15 minutes

---

3 courgettes (total weight about 500g / 1lb 2oz)

1 egg, lightly beaten

3 tablespoons finely chopped mint leaves

100g (3½oz) feta cheese, crumbled

couple of pinches of chilli flakes (optional)

75g (2¾oz) chickpea (gram) flour

3–4 tablespoons olive oil

sea salt flakes and freshly ground black pepper

Tzatziki (see overleaf), to serve

Coarsely grate the courgettes, then squeeze out as much water as possible by putting them in a clean tea towel and wringing them out as hard as you can.

Mix the squeezed courgette with the egg in a large mixing bowl with the mint, feta, salt and pepper, and a little chilli, if you like.

Once well mixed, add the chickpea flour until the consistency is such that you can form small sloppy balls of mixture, each roughly the size of a walnut.

Pour 2 tablespoons of the oil in a large frying pan over a medium-low heat. As you form each patty, drop it gently into the pan and fry for 3–4 minutes on each side, until nicely browned and crisp outside and cooked within (you may need to press and shape each fritter a little with a spatula as you cook it). You should be able to cook around 6 fritters in each batch.

Keep the first batch warm on a plate covered with foil while you cook the rest, adding more oil as you cook, if you need it. Serve the fritters warm, with a bowl of Tzatziki.

Tzatziki

Quick and easy to prepare, this super-simple accompaniment is rarely absent from our table throughout the summer months, though it's no stranger in winter either! Thick Greek yogurt, lovely fresh cucumbers, a hit of raw garlic and a hint of zingy mint, it's perfect with almost any barbecued or roast meat and is lapped up with gusto by the non-meat eaters as well. Delicious when dipped into with toasted pitta, or as an accompaniment to my Courgette Fritters with Mint & Feta (see page 179).

Feeds 6–8

Preparation time: 5 minutes

1 large cucumber

500g (1lb 2oz) Greek yogurt (low-fat if you insist, but the proper 10 per cent fat stuff just tastes nicer!)

1–2 garlic cloves, crushed

leaves from ½ small bunch of mint (about 15g / ½oz), chopped, plus more shredded leaves to serve

finely grated zest and juice of 1 lemon

sea salt flakes and freshly ground black pepper

extra virgin olive oil, to serve

Coarsely grate the cucumber.

Tip the yogurt into a large mixing bowl. Add the garlic, chopped mint, lemon juice, salt and pepper. Mix well, then stir in the cucumber. Taste and adjust the seasoning if necessary.

Transfer to a serving bowl and top off with lemon zest, shredded mint leaves and a drizzle of olive oil.

Salsa verde

The joy of a salsa verde is that you can experiment with different quantities and types of ingredients to end up with the right balance of flavours and crucial tanginess. You want a good level of piquancy, but not so much that it overshadows the delicious herbs. The peppery earthiness of parsley makes it a must, but you can vary the levels of basil and mint according to how much you like their flavours. You can easily make tweaks and substitutes too – for example, swap the garlic for shallots, the capers for gherkins, or use lemon juice instead of vinegar. Err on the side of making too much, as salsa verde is equally good with cold meats and pretty much anything else you put it on.

Makes enough for 12 servings (scale down if needed)

Preparation time: 10 minutes

---

large bunch of flat leaf parsley (about 60g / 2¼oz)

large bunch of basil (about 60g / 2¼oz)

large handful of mint leaves (about 30 leaves)

4 garlic cloves

50g (1¾oz) tin of anchovy fillets in olive oil, drained

4 tablespoons baby capers, rinsed if salted, drained if in brine

2 tablespoons Dijon mustard

4 tablespoons red wine vinegar

200ml (7fl oz) extra virgin olive oil, plus more if needed

sea salt flakes and freshly ground black pepper

Roughly chop the first five ingredients and put into the bowl of a mini food processor. Or, if you prefer a more textured finish and want to keep the vibrant colours of the herbs, you can do the whole thing without a food processor, just finely chop the first five ingredients and stir in the rest.

If using the food processor, add half the capers, the mustard and vinegar and season with salt and pepper. Whizz for a few seconds.

Gradually add the oil to make a spoonable sauce, adding a little more if the mixture is too stiff. Sprinkle over the remaining capers and whizz (if using a mini processor) for just 3–4 seconds more to combine.

Green beans with hazelnuts

This fresh, vibrant dish is good on the table as part of a selection, if you've got a few people over. It can easily be prepared in advance. This recipe is my version of one in our favourite Ottolenghi cookbook, tweaked over the years.

Feeds 6

Preparation time: 10 minutes

Cooking time: 5 minutes

500g (1lb 2oz) green beans, with stalks nipped off

100g (3½oz) blanched hazelnuts

2 tablespoons extra virgin olive oil

finely grated zest and juice of 1 lemon or orange

sea salt flakes and freshly ground black pepper

Half-fill a large saucepan with water and bring to the boil. Toss in your green beans. Cook for 5 minutes, then tip into a sieve or colander. Immediately run under cold water until the beans are stone-cold. Leave to drain.

Meanwhile, toast the hazelnuts in a frying pan, tossing occasionally until lightly browned. Tip on to a work surface and roughly chop, or bash with a rolling pin.

Transfer the beans to a serving dish, toss with the olive oil, lemon or orange zest and juice, salt and pepper. Finally, sprinkle over the toasted hazelnuts.

Charlie's tip It adds a bit of hassle, but I also make this using hazelnuts in their skins, instead of blanched nuts. You will end up with some tasty bits of nut that are almost burnt, but they add some extra flavour. If you decide to try this, you'll need to toast the nuts in a dry frying pan. You want the skins to turn very dark brown, so watch them carefully and turn often. Once the hazelnuts are toasted, transfer to a tea towel and give them a good rub to loosen most of the husks. Discard the husks, then bash gently with a rolling pin.

Tenderstem broccoli with garlic & chilli

OK, this is not a complicated recipe, but I reckon it's one of the best ways to eat broccoli and is super-quick and easy. Of course you can make it with regular broccoli (or the rather exotic purple-sprouting), but I'm a fan of Tenderstem, which is actually a hybrid of broccoli and kale. This is a great green veg dish to go with almost anything; if spicy doesn't fit, just leave out the chilli.

Feeds 6
Preparation time: 5 minutes
Cooking time: 10 minutes

olive oil

500g (1lb 2oz) Tenderstem broccoli, stalks trimmed

5 garlic cloves, roughly chopped

1–2 red chillies, depending on your spice tolerance, deseeded and sliced into matchsticks

50g (1¾oz) flaked almonds

sea salt flakes and freshly ground black pepper

Heat a glug of olive oil in a large frying pan or wok over a high heat until it is nice and hot, then toss in the broccoli and cook for about 5 minutes. It's fine if it chars a little bit in places, but don't let it burn, keep it moving a bit in the pan.

Add the garlic and chillies and another splash of olive oil if the pan looks dry. Season with salt and pepper. Cook for a couple of minutes, stirring.

Finally, add the flaked almonds and cook for a final couple of minutes, allowing them to toast just a little.

Charlie's tip Give this dish an extra layer of flavour by whisking a couple of tablespoons of tahini with twice as much water, then drizzling the thick liquid over the broccoli.

Roast jerusalem artichokes with garlic & pancetta

You may not find Jerusalem artichokes in your local supermarket, but do keep an eye out for them in greengrocers and farm shops because they are very tasty. They look nothing like a globe artichoke, more a cross between a piece of root ginger and a small potato, and their two downsides are that they can be a bit of a fiddle to clean and peel, and they are sometimes known as 'fartichokes' for a good reason! Don't let either downside put you off giving them a try. They make a very tasty soup (follow the same idea as the Butternut Squash Soup with Chilli & Pine Nuts on page 40, if you want to give this a go) and they also roast well.

Feeds 5–6

Preparation time: 10 minutes

Cooking time: 30 minutes

600g (1lb 5oz) Jerusalem artichokes

3–4 tablespoons olive oil

5 garlic cloves, finely chopped

a few thyme sprigs

100g (3½oz) diced pancetta

sea salt flakes and freshly ground black pepper

Preheat the oven to 200°C/180°C fan (400°F), Gas Mark 6.

Prepare your artichokes. Some people are happy to leave the skins on (in which case give them a very thorough wash and scrub) while others, like me, prefer to peel them. Cut into thick slices, or cut in half lengthways if small.

Scatter the prepared artichokes into a roasting tin, then add a little seasoning. Drizzle the whole lot with a generous glug of olive oil, then roast in the hot oven for 15 minutes.

Add the garlic, thyme and pancetta to the roasting tin and give it all a good muddle to make sure the artichokes are cooking evenly and are nicely coated in olive oil. Roast for a further 15 minutes, or until the artichokes are softened and the pancetta is lightly browned.

Fennel with honey & pine nuts

I love fennel; in my view it's an underused vegetable. This is my go-to fennel recipe, nice and easy to prepare with a wonderful sweetness and just the merest hint of aniseed. You can either serve it warm, or it's equally delicious at room temperature as part of a big spread. This goes especially well with Slow-Cooked Shoulder of Lamb with Marmite, or Boneless Whole Chickens with Two Marinades (see pages 146 and 129).

Feeds 6
Preparation time: 5 minutes
Cooking time: 35 minutes

---

4 fennel bulbs

4 tablespoons olive oil, plus more for the baking tray

juice of 1 lemon

2 tablespoons runny honey

25g (1oz) pine nuts

sea salt flakes

chopped parsley leaves, to serve

Preheat the oven to 220°C/200°C fan (425°F), Gas Mark 7.

Trim the fennel – take off any excess root, being careful to leave enough to keep the bulbs intact. Trim off the green tops of the fennel and keep for later. Slice the fennel lengthways into pieces just under 1cm (½ inch) thick (each bulb should give around 6 slices).

Lay the fennel in a single layer in a very large, lightly oiled baking tray. Drizzle over the olive oil and sprinkle with a small amount of salt. Bake for around 20 minutes.

Remove the fennel from the oven, carefully flip it over, taking care to leave it as whole pieces, then pour over the lemon juice and drizzle over the honey. Return to the oven for 10–12 minutes, or until softened and lightly browned.

Meanwhile, toast the pine nuts in a small frying pan, being careful not to burn them – something I'm renowned for in our house!

Once cooked, carefully lift the fennel from the baking tray and place on a serving dish. Sprinkle with the toasted pine nuts, parsley and reserved fennel tops.

Roast aubergines with garlic & herbs

This dish couldn't really be more simple, but it always goes down well. It is great as part of a spread as well as a side dish, for example with my Griddled Squid with a Tomato-Pepper Salsa (see page 89), perhaps for lunch outside on a nice sunny day. I love aubergines and nearly always have a few in my fridge. Years ago, there used to be a whole ritual of salting aubergines to remove their bitter juices, but luckily modern varieties mean this is no longer required and they are now quick to prepare. Aubergines are very absorbent and pretty thirsty; they will soak up a lot of oil. My preference is to cook them dry and add the olive oil afterwards.

Feeds 6

Preparation time: 5 minutes

Cooking time: 15 minutes

2 large aubergines (total weight about 600g / 1lb 5oz)

4–6 garlic cloves, depending on size, crushed (I am a garlic fan and use even more than this; you may want to tone it down)

20g (¾oz) chopped herbs (I like a mix of thyme, oregano and parsley)

6–7 tablespoons extra virgin olive oil

finely grated zest and juice of ½ lemon

sea salt flakes and freshly ground black pepper

Slice the aubergines lengthways into thin strips – aim for about 5mm (¼ inch) thick.

Cook the slices in batches on a very hot griddle pan or barbecue, around 2 minutes on each side should do it (a little longer if your slices are thicker). You may need to do this in batches.

Once all the aubergines are cooked, arrange on a serving dish. Sprinkle with the garlic, to taste, chopped herbs and generous amounts of salt and pepper, then add the olive oil and muddle together. Sprinkle with the lemon juice and scatter over the lemon zest to finish.

Parsnips with garlic, thyme & honey

As we slide into autumn and winter, root vegetables come into their own and parsnips are among my favourites. Here's a nice easy way to cook them to make a great accompaniment to almost any meat dish, or they are also delicious on their own. If you wanted to elevate these to a stand-alone dish, I'd suggest crumbling some feta over the top along with a sprinkling of toasted and chopped hazelnuts.

Feeds 6
Preparation time: 5 minutes
Cooking time: 35–45 minutes

500g (1lb 2oz) parsnips, peeled

2–3 tablespoons olive oil

3 garlic cloves, finely sliced

1 tablespoon thyme leaves

3 tablespoons runny honey, plus a drizzle at the end

sea salt flakes and freshly ground black pepper

Preheat the oven to 220°C/200°C fan (425°F), Gas Mark 7.

Cut the parsnips in half, put them flat-side down on a work surface and cut into long strips about 1cm (½ inch) thick.

Put a decent glug of olive oil into a baking tray, then tumble in the prepared parsnips. Season with salt and pepper. Cook in the hot oven for 15 minutes.

Add the garlic, thyme and honey, turn the parsnips over and give them a bit of a muddle to ensure they are coated and will cook evenly. Return to the oven for another 20–30 minutes, until the parsnips are slightly browned and sticky, turning them over once more towards the end to ensure they are evenly coated in the honey mixture.

Roast beets with rosemary & chard

Quick and simple. If you can, it's fun to use a mix of both purple and golden beetroot, and if you have a choice, I'd recommend going for smaller beets. For the chard, use what you can find, any colour or thickness of stems; just cut the thicker stems smaller so they cook evenly. This dish works well with a weekend roast, or give them a go with my Red Pepper & Goats' Cheese Tart, or the Sausage & Puy Lentil Casserole (see pages 64 and 112).

Feeds 6

Preparation time: 5 minutes

Cooking time: 30 minutes

500g (1lb 2oz) raw beetroot

50ml (3½ tablespoons) olive oil

small bunch of rosemary

3 garlic cloves, roughly chopped

200g (7oz) chard, roughly chopped

sea salt flakes

Preheat the oven to 220°C/200°C fan (425°F), Gas Mark 7.

Wash the beetroot (no need to peel and don't worry if there are a few root hairs still visible; just leave them on), then cut into quarters or large chunks.

Toss the prepared beetroot, olive oil and rosemary into a large roasting tin with a pinch of salt and then muddle together, ensuring all the beetroot has got a light coating of oil.

Cook in the hot oven for 30 minutes, adding the garlic and give the roasting tin a good shake halfway through. Five minutes before the end of cooking, or when the beetroot is almost tender, add the roughly chopped chard and muddle together with the beetroot. Continue cooking until the chard has wilted, then taste and add a little more salt, if needed.

Savoy cabbage with chestnuts

When it comes to cabbage these days, it seems most chefs have fallen in love with the Hispi, and it's not bad at all, especially roasted over a fire, then slathered in tasty dressing or sauce. But I'm a fan of the good old Savoy, readily available and inexpensive and pretty easy to grow too. Add a few chestnuts and a generous amount of butter and, with next-to-zero effort, you've got a lovely green winter veg dish that will go well with any roast, or with a baked Vacherin cheese and some good crusty bread.

Feeds 4–6
Preparation time: 5 minutes
Cooking time: 10 minutes

---

1 large Savoy cabbage

100g (3½oz) unsweetened, shelled chestnuts (I like the Merchant Gourmet brand)

40g (1½oz) butter

sea salt flakes and freshly ground black pepper

Cut the cabbage in half and trim off the woody stalk and any manky outer leaves. Slice the cabbage about 1cm (½ inch) thick and steam or cook in a large saucepan of boiling water until tender (4–5 minutes).

Meanwhile, crumble or chop the chestnuts into smallish pieces.

Once the cabbage is cooked, drain in a colander, then put the butter, chestnuts, a pinch or so of salt and a generous amount of pepper in the pan and heat until the butter begins to sizzle.

Return the cabbage to the pan and toss well together. Serve immediately.

Charlie's tip This chapter is all about veg, but this particular dish is also good with fried bacon lardons stirred in.

Braised radicchio with balsamic & honey

I've always had a bit of a soft spot for radicchio and its close (and easier to find) relation, red chicory. I like their bitterness and beautiful colour. In Italy they are usually eaten cooked, which reduces the bitterness slightly – but not too much – and this recipe works well, as you get some lovely sweetness both from the balsamic vinegar and, of course, the honey. The dish makes a good accompaniment to red meat.

Feeds 6
Preparation time: 5 minutes
Cooking time: 25 minutes

4–5 heads of radicchio or red chicory, outer leaves removed

4 tablespoons olive oil

5 tablespoons balsamic vinegar

3 tablespoons runny honey

leaves from 2 thyme sprigs (I like lemon thyme)

sea salt flakes and freshly ground black pepper

Cut the radicchio or chicory in half, then into wedges, about 3 wedges per half.

Heat the olive oil in a large frying pan that has a lid, then put in the radicchio or chicory wedges cut-side down and cook over a medium heat for just 2–3 minutes.

Add the balsamic vinegar, then enough water to lie about 1cm (½ inch) deep in the pan. Drizzle over the honey, sprinkle with salt, grind over some pepper and scatter over your thyme leaves.

Put the lid on the pan and simmer over a low heat for around 20 minutes, or until the radicchio or chicory is tender, turning them over halfway, so they cook evenly.

Once the radicchio or chicory is cooked, remove it from the pan to a plate. Increase the heat and reduce the remaining liquid to a thin syrup. Return the radicchio or chicory to the pan, if it's good enough to serve it in, or place on a serving plate, then pour the syrup over and serve.

Charlie's tip Radicchio and chicory go particularly well with blue cheese, so if you're as partial to it as I am, then you might like to put a bit over the top. Gorgonzola or Dolcelatte would be perfect for this quintessentially Italian vegetable, but any blue cheese should work.

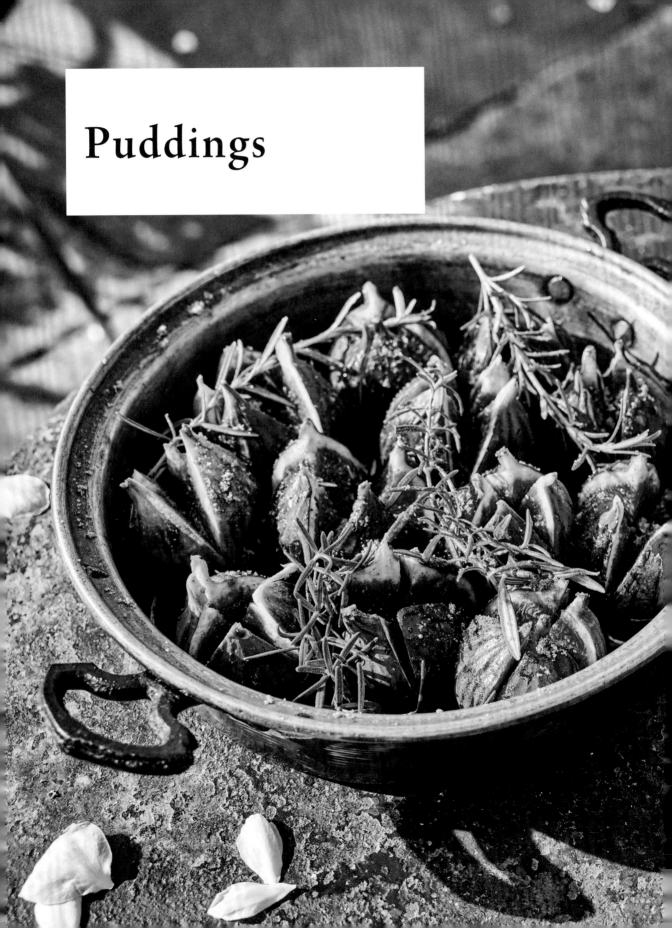

Puddings

Poached pears for summer

Poached pears are such an easy, delicious and elegant pudding that they deserve not one but two recipes: a summer and a winter version. My summer poached pears are delicate and subtle with a strong Persian influence and are best served cold.

Feeds 6

Preparation time: 10 minutes, plus at least 1 hour, and up to overnight, cooling and chilling

Cooking time: 20 minutes

---

6 firm Conference pears

bottle of inexpensive white wine

175g (6oz) caster sugar

generous pinch of saffron threads

20 cardamom pods, lightly crushed

2 vanilla pods, split in half lengthways, seeds removed

To serve

300ml (½ pint) double cream

seeds from 1 vanilla pod (from the pods used above)

dash of rose water

leaves from 1 lemon thyme sprig

Peel the pears, leaving the stalks on. Cut off the bases so they are flat and the pears will stand up on their own.

Lay the pears down in a large saucepan (they don't need to stand up at this point), then add all the other ingredients, including the vanilla pods, but not their seeds. Heat until just short of boiling, then reduce the heat and leave to simmer for 15 minutes, turning the pears over half way through if they aren't covered in syrup.

Remove the pan from the heat and leave the pears to cool in their syrup; you want this to be about the consistency of a thick cordial, so boil it to reduce, if necessary.

If possible, make the pears up to this stage in advance, put them in a container to cool, then refrigerate, covered, overnight. Bring them up to room temperature before serving.

When you are ready to serve, carefully place the pears standing up on individual flat plates or in shallow bowls with some of the cooled cooking syrup poured over and around them.

Whip the cream, vanilla seeds and rose water to soft peaks, then serve with the pears, scattering with a touch of lemon thyme leaves.

Poached pears for winter

As a contrast to my summer pears, my warm winter poached pears are robust, dark and unctuous: perfect for a cold winter's day. Delicious with ice cream or crème fraîche.

Feeds 6

Preparation time: 10 minutes, plus at least 1 hour cooling

Cooking time: 45 minutes

---

6 firm Conference pears

bottle of inexpensive red wine

175g (6oz) Demerara sugar

8 cloves

1 cinnamon stick

generous thumb-sized piece of root ginger, cut into matchsticks

thyme sprig

Peel the pears, leaving the stalks on. Cut off the bases so they are flat and the pears will stand up on their own.

Lay the pears down in your saucepan (they don't need to stand up at this point), then add all the other ingredients. Heat until just short of boiling, then reduce the heat and leave to simmer for 30 minutes.

Remove from the heat and leave the pears to cool in the syrup for at least 1 hour so they absorb the flavours and turn a rich maroon, then remove them from the pan and set them aside.

Now heat up the remaining liquid in the saucepan over a high heat and boil for 10–15 minutes, or until thickened to a golden syrup-like consistency.

When you are ready to serve, carefully place the pears standing up on individual flat plates or shallow bowls, or place them all on a large, flat serving dish if you prefer to bring a bit of theatre to the table, I usually do! Pour over the syrup, warming it up first, if you need to.

Charlie's tip You can adjust your spices, to taste, adding a couple of star anise to the syrup, for instance.

Baked figs with spiced honey & ricotta

Sometimes you just want something simple for pudding. I love figs and they tend to be readily available in the late summer and autumn, a time of year when they are also good value. A fresh fig picked off the tree is a delight in itself (and probably best eaten straight away), but shop-bought figs tend to be smaller, have slightly thicker skins and are easily elevated by a quick burst in the oven with a few other flavours thrown in that show them to their best advantage.

Feeds 6
Preparation time: 5 minutes
Cooking time: 25–30 minutes

50g (1¾oz) light muscovado sugar

1 teaspoon ground cinnamon

12 figs

50ml (3½ tablespoons) Madeira, or other sweetish booze you have spare

4 rosemary sprigs

250g (9oz) ricotta cheese

100g (3½oz) walnut halves

4 tablespoons runny honey

Preheat the oven to 200°C/180°C fan (400°F), Gas Mark 6.

Mix together the sugar and cinnamon in a small mixing bowl. Starting at the stem end, cut the figs halfway down in a cross shape.

Arrange your cut figs in a single layer in a baking dish and sprinkle the cut surfaces with the sugar and cinnamon. Sprinkle with the Madeira and then toss the rosemary sprigs on top before baking for 25–30 minutes, or until the figs are soft and the juices have run to make a delicious sauce.

Once the cooked figs come out of the oven, spoon clumps of your ricotta over the top, scatter on the nuts and drizzle the whole dish with the honey. Best served warm.

Charlie's tip To really bring out their flavour, you can lightly toast the walnuts in the oven for five minutes while the figs are cooking, but don't forget them! Leave them to cool before breaking over the figs.

Frangipane cherry tart

Frangipane is cooking alchemy: combine almonds, sugar and butter in equal quantities and the result is just delicious. It provides the perfect base for a whole variety of fruits and I use it with apples, pears, apricots and peaches. But perhaps my favourite with frangipane is cherries; that's why one of our Charlie Bigham's puddings is our cherry bakewell. This recipe takes its inspiration from that, but with a pastry tart base.

Feeds 8–10

Preparation time: 30 minutes, plus 30 minutes chilling

Cooking time: 60–70 minutes

For the pastry

175g (6oz) plain flour, plus more to dust

50g (1¾oz) icing sugar, sifted

90g (3¼oz) chilled butter, cut into small pieces

1 egg yolk

1 tablespoon ice-cold water

fine sea salt

For the filling

175g (6oz) butter, softened

175g (6oz) caster sugar

175g (6oz) ground almonds

2 large eggs

350g (12oz) cherries (I tend to use frozen and defrosted or canned and drained, but pitted fresh cherries are also delicious)

3 tablespoons flaked almonds

For the pastry, sift the flour, icing sugar and a pinch of salt into a food processor. Add the butter and whizz until the mixture looks like fine crumbs, then tip into a mixing bowl. Alternatively, rub the butter into the flour in a mixing bowl, then stir in the icing sugar.

In a small bowl, beat the egg yolk with the cold water. Add the yolk mixture to the flour and bring together into a ball. Turn out on to a floured work surface and knead briefly until smooth. Wrap in clingfilm and chill for 30 minutes, then roll out thinly on a lightly floured work surface and use to line a 25cm (10 inch) fluted tart tin with a removable base.

Preheat the oven to 200°C/180°C fan (400°F), Gas Mark 6.

Line the tart case with a sheet of nonstick baking paper and cover with baking beans. Put the pastry case on a baking sheet and bake for around 10 minutes. Remove the paper and baking beans and cook for another 2–3 minutes, or until the base is no longer wet-looking. Remove from the oven and allow to cool.

Reduce the oven temperature to 180°C/160°C fan (350°F), Gas Mark 4.

For the filling, mix the butter and sugar together in a food processor, or with electric beaters in a large mixing bowl, until pale and fluffy, then add the almonds and finally the eggs, one at a time.

Spoon the frangipane on top of the pastry and spread out evenly. Arrange the cherries on top and push down slightly into the frangipane. Bake for about 30 minutes, turning the tart at the halfway stage to ensure it is evenly cooked.

Scatter over the flaked almonds and return to the oven for another 15–20 minutes until golden.

Charlie's tip Before spreading the frangipane over the tart base, you could add a layer of cherry compote or jam.

Nectarine tarte tatin

A classic pudding. I will often knock up a tarte Tatin if I need a pud and haven't got a lot of time. An apple tarte Tatin is the true classic – and very good it is too – but you can experiment with different fruit. Pear is great; banana works well too, strangely. Here I've gone for nectarine as they are available pretty much all year round but are not necessarily tasty out of their high season in July and August. Cooking them with a bit of caramel makes all the difference, and they look gorgeous too.

Feeds 6

Preparation time: 10 minutes, plus 10 minutes cooling

Cooking time: 35 minutes

75g (2¾oz) caster sugar

40g (1½oz) butter, cubed

2 tablespoons brandy, or lemon juice

4–5 ripe nectarines, halved and pitted

325g (11½oz) sheet of ready-rolled puff pastry (ideally all-butter), defrosted if frozen

plain flour, to dust

crème fraîche, cream or ice cream, to serve

Sprinkle the sugar over a small ovenproof frying pan or tarte Tatin tin, which measures roughly 20cm (8 inches) across its base. Place over a medium heat and cook until the sugar first melts and then caramelises and turns a rich golden brown. Don't stir the sugar too much as it melts, but swirl the pan as it changes colour; this whole process will take 4–5 minutes. Be careful it doesn't burn.

Remove the caramel from the heat and stir in the butter with a wooden spoon. Watch out, as the caramel will be extremely hot. Be careful of any splashes and do not be tempted to taste it at any stage! Next add the brandy or lemon juice. Continue stirring for 2 minutes as the caramel cools and thickens.

When the caramel is smooth, carefully arrange the nectarines on top, cut-sides down. Leave to cool for 10 minutes.

Unroll the puff pastry on its paper and sprinkle lightly with flour. With a rolling pin, roll to increase the width to about 28cm (11 inches). Find a plate that is that diameter and use it as a template, cutting the pastry around the plate and lifting off the trimmings. (These can be used to make some tasty cheese straws, no need for good pastry to go to waste!)

Prick the pastry lightly with a fork a few times, lift the sheet over a floured rolling pin and gently drop it on top of the nectarines. Tuck the edges in around the fruit. Cook immediately, or leave to cool and then chill overnight, taking it out of the fridge 45 minutes before you want to bake it.

Preheat the oven to 220°C/fan 200°C (425°F), Gas Mark 7. Bake the tarte Tatin for around 25 minutes, or until the pastry is risen and golden brown. Take out of the oven using an oven cloth to hold the pan; it will be extremely hot.

Stand for no more than 2–3 minutes to allow the tarte to settle, then loosen the edges with a palette knife and place a large serving plate on top of the pan. Very carefully flip it over, using a folded tea towel to help you hold the pan, and allow the tarte to drop gently on to the plate. Serve warm with crème fraîche, cream or ice cream.

Sticky ginger pudding

Who doesn't love a sticky toffee pudding? At Charlie Bigham's, we make one that can hold its own against the very best, but when it comes to cooking it at home, I love to add a bit of ginger to give it a little kick. As well as ground ginger, I also use stem ginger here, one of those ingredients that's always worth having in your storecupboard.

Feeds 8–10

Preparation time: 10 minutes

Cooking time: 35 minutes

175g (6oz) chopped pitted dates

60g (2¼oz) butter, softened, plus more for the tin

120g (4¼oz) self-raising flour

3 teaspoons ground ginger

½ teaspoon bicarbonate of soda

130g (4¾oz) dark muscovado sugar

2 eggs

40g (1½oz) golden syrup

40g (1½oz) stem ginger in syrup, drained and finely chopped

fine sea salt

crème fraîche or whipped cream, to serve

For the sauce

80g (2¾oz) butter

100g (3½oz) dark muscovado sugar

30g (1oz) black treacle

50g (1¾oz) stem ginger in syrup, drained and finely chopped

1 teaspoon vanilla extract

300ml (½ pint) double cream

4 tablespoons of syrup from the ginger jar

Put the dates in a heatproof bowl and cover with about 200ml (7fl oz) of boiling water. Allow to sit for 10 minutes, then drain.

Preheat the oven to 200°C/180°C fan (400°F), Gas Mark 6. Butter a 20cm (8 inch) cake tin.

Sift the flour into a mixing bowl with the ground ginger, bicarbonate of soda and a pinch of salt.

Combine your butter and sugar in a stand mixer, or with a mixing bowl and electric beaters. While beating, add 1 egg, then half the flour mixture, then add the second egg followed by the remaining flour mixture, then add the golden syrup. Once well mixed, fold in your soaked, drained dates and chopped stem ginger.

Pour the mix into the prepared tin and bake for 30–35 minutes, or until a skewer comes out clean from the centre. You can leave this to cool completely, or serve it warm with the sauce.

To make your sauce, melt the butter in a saucepan, then add the sugar, treacle, stem ginger, vanilla extract and cream with the ginger syrup. Cook over a low heat until all the sugar has dissolved and you have a good dark sauce.

Serve slices of the pudding with your ginger toffee sauce and crème fraîche or whipped cream.

Brioche summer pudding

This is among the first puddings I ever made. I hadn't made it for a few years and decided to give it another go to see if it was still as good as I remembered – let's face it, the idea of a random bunch of fruit and some slightly stale bread doesn't necessarily sound that tasty! And yes, this is actually a delicious pudding, as well as incredibly easy to make. Bear in mind that you need a little advance planning as this is best made 24 hours in advance (and 48 hours is even better). I've always made it with fresh fruit and of course fresh is always best. However, it's very nearly as good made with frozen fruit and this is one of those instances when you can save yourself a bit of money and maybe nobody will ever know, though I've suggested adding some fresh fruit on top to assist the subterfuge!

Feeds 8

Preparation time: 10 minutes, plus at least 24 hours resting

Cooking time: 5 minutes

1kg (2lb 4oz) mixed frozen berries

200g (7oz) caster sugar

100ml (3½fl oz) water

550–600g (1lb 4oz–1lb 5oz) sliced brioche

100g (3½oz) fresh fruit, such as raspberries, strawberries, blackcurrants, redcurrants or blackberries, whatever you have to hand, to decorate

whipped cream or crème fraîche, to serve

Line a 1.8–2 litre (3–3½ pint) pudding bowl with clingfilm. Tip the frozen fruit into a large saucepan along with the sugar and water and warm over a low heat, stirring occasionally, until the fruit has defrosted and softened and the sugar dissolved. Drain off the juice through a sieve into a large bowl.

Slice off the crusts from the brioche. Dip the slices on both sides in the fruit juices and use these to line your prepared pudding bowl, ensuring that the surface is covered by the bread with no gaps between the slices.

Tip the fruit into the bread-lined bowl and then cover with a layer of juice-dipped bread; again, no gaps! Pour any remaining juice over the top.

Find a plate that is just a little smaller in diameter than the bowl. Put it into the bowl, then put a heavy weight on the plate. Leave the weighted bowl in the fridge for at least 24 hours and up to 48 hours.

When you are ready to eat, use a palette knife to loosen the bread from the bowl. Place a flattish serving dish with a small rim on top of the bowl, then turn everything over to tip out the pudding.

Serve with some fresh fruit scattered over the top, with a generous lashing of whipped cream or crème fraîche.

Charlie's tip If you can make this 48 hours in advance, it will taste just that bit better, as the juices seep even more into the bread and the whole pudding matures in flavour.

Lemon & poppy seed madeleines

There's something so beautiful about a madeleine; when you see them on a plate, you just want to eat them. They can easily be elevated to something a little more sophisticated by serving with some fresh fruit – I suggest strawberries – and whipped cream laced with a little vanilla. You do need a special tin to make a proper scallop-shaped madeleine, but if you don't have one, then use a mince pie tin to create some madeleine-ish cakes – not quite as elegant, but still tasty. The classic recipe is plain, but I think the addition of lemon and poppy seeds takes these lovely morsels to a higher level.

Makes 20–24

Preparation time: 10 minutes, plus 1–12 hours chilling

Cooking time: 10 minutes

90g (3¼oz) butter, plus more for the tins

2 eggs

60g (2¼oz) caster sugar

30g (1oz) Demerara sugar

2 teaspoons runny honey

finely grated zest of 1 lemon

1 tablespoon poppy seeds

90g (3¼oz) plain flour, plus more for the tins

½ teaspoon baking powder

To serve (optional)

icing sugar, to decorate

strawberries

whipped double cream

vanilla seeds, or vanilla extract

Melt the butter in a small saucepan over a medium heat. Set aside to cool.

Put the eggs in a large mixing bowl with the caster and Demerara sugars, then whisk with electric beaters until roughly tripled in volume. Mix in the honey, lemon zest and poppy seeds, followed by the now-cooled butter.

Sift the flour and baking powder into the bowl, then gently fold into the egg mixture. Cover and put in the fridge for at least 1 hour and up to 12.

Meanwhile, generously grease 2 madeleine tins with more butter and lightly dust with flour. Ideally stick these into the fridge as well.

When you're ready to bake, preheat the oven to 200°C/180°C fan (400°F), Gas Mark 6.

Spoon 1 tablespoon of your chilled batter into each madeleine mould.

Bake the madeleines in the oven for about 8 minutes, keeping a careful eye on them to ensure they don't burn. Once cooked, allow to cool in the tin for a minute or so, then tip out on to a wire rack.

Sift over a little icing sugar and serve with strawberries and whipped cream laced with vanilla, or even just with a cup of tea for elevenses, or as a mid-afternoon pick-me-up.

Florentines

Deceptively simple, but so much better than anything you will ever find in a shop, these tasty biscuits can be merrily tucked into at any time of the day and make a simple end to a meal when perhaps a full-on pudding is too much. Although French in origin rather than Italian, I think it's appropriate they are named after one of Italy's loveliest cities as I always associate that part of Italy with candied peel, which is at the heart of every good florentine. My daughter Petra is the Florentine Queen in our house and makes them with much more care and precision than I ever would; these are, without doubt, the best florentines I've ever tasted.

Makes about 20

Preparation time: 10 minutes, plus cooling

Cooking time: 10–12 minutes

100g (3½oz) flaked almonds

30g (1oz) shelled unsalted pistachios, roughly chopped

100g (3½oz) candied peel

50g (1¾oz) dried cranberries

70g (2½oz) plain flour

85g (3oz) butter, cut into cubes

100g (3½oz) light muscovado sugar

50g (1¾oz) golden syrup

1 tablespoon double cream

pinch of sea salt flakes

200g (7oz) dark chocolate (I'd recommend no stronger than 70 per cent cocoa solids), chopped

Preheat the oven to 180°C/160°C fan (350°F), Gas Mark 4. Line 2 baking trays with nonstick baking paper.

Put the nuts, peel and cranberries in a mixing bowl. Sift over the flour and mix everything together well so the flour coats the fruit and nuts evenly.

Put the cubed butter, sugar and golden syrup into a medium-large saucepan and cook over a low heat, stirring constantly, until melted. Immediately remove from the heat and stir in the cream and a pinch of salt, then thoroughly mix in the floury fruit and nuts.

Use a tablespoon to measure your florentine mix on to the prepared trays, a generous spoonful at a time, to create round florentine blobs. Leave lots of space between each, as they will expand more than you think when you cook them.

Cook the florentines for 10–12 minutes, until lightly browned and bubbling. Remove from the oven and leave to cool on the tray for 5–10 minutes, then transfer to a wire rack to cool completely.

Bring a little water to a simmer in a small saucepan and find a heatproof bowl that will fit on top without touching the water. Put your chocolate in the heatproof bowl and place over the simmering water. Melt the chocolate.

Spread the base of the cooled florentines with the chocolate using a knife or palette knife, then leave to dry and set for a few hours. For a professional finish, you can run a fork over the warm chocolate as it sets, to create beautiful grooves.

Hunza apricots with whipped pistachio cream

Hunza apricots are not just any old apricot – they come from a remote valley in the mountains of Pakistan and have a flavour all of their own. There is some evidence to say that these trees, growing in the Hindu Kush, are the source of all apricot trees around the world. You won't find a Hunza apricot in a supermarket, but you should be able to track them down in specialist delis or health food shops. If they are proving elusive, you can also order them online (they are often sold in 1kg / 2lb 4oz bags, but don't worry, they keep for a good long time and you will want to eat them all). I think they make a very tasty and rather unusual quick pudding.

Feeds 4

Preparation time: 5 minutes

Cooking time: 10 minutes

200g (7oz) Hunza apricots

200ml (7fl oz) water

100ml (3½oz) double cream

30g (1oz) shelled unsalted pistachios

Tip the apricots into a small saucepan, add the water and cook over a medium-high heat for about 10 minutes, stirring occasionally and ensuring they don't boil dry. You are aiming to reduce the water to almost nothing, just leaving a few tablespoons of liquid that will have thickened to make a thin syrup.

Once the apricots are cooked, remove the pan from the heat and leave them to cool in the liquid.

For the pistachio cream, whip the cream to soft peaks in a mixing bowl, using a whisk or electric beaters. Put the nuts into a clean tea towel and use a rolling pin to smash them into pieces (not too small). Reserve a handful for decoration and stir the rest into your whipped cream.

The apricots can be served either warm (my preference) or cold. Serve in small bowls with a spoonful of the juice poured over the top of them, with a generous blob of whipped pistachio cream and extra pistachios. When you eat the apricots, the joy is in sucking the last of the fruit off the stones: pure nectar!

Lemon posset with cantuccini

We all need a lemon pudding in our repertoire. Which to choose for this book? It was a tough call and I've had to leave both a rich lemon tart and a lemon polenta cake on the cutting-room floor in favour of the simplicity of a lemon posset. Just three ingredients and barely ten minutes are all it takes to make a pudding that delivers a lot. With the simple addition of cantuccini – Italian almond biscuits – it's a certain crowd-pleaser.

Feeds 6

Preparation time: 10 minutes, plus at least 3 hours setting

Cooking time: 5 minutes

---

finely grated zest and juice of 2–3 unwaxed lemons, plus finely grated zest of 1 extra lemon to serve

8 cantuccini

600ml (20fl oz) double cream

150g (5½oz) caster sugar

Measure out 80ml (5½ tablespoons) of lemon juice, squeezing the third lemon if necessary.

Bash 2 of the cantuccini with a rolling pin to make crumbs and set aside.

Pour the cream into a saucepan, add the sugar and slowly bring to the boil, stirring all the while to ensure the sugar dissolves. Simmer for 1 minute.

Remove from the heat, then add the lemon juice and half the zest. Your mixture should start to thicken. Taste, then add as much more of the zest as you need: you want your posset to be sweet, tangy and creamy, but all tastes will differ a little on this.

Pour the mixture into a jug and leave to cool for 10 minutes or so, then pour into 6 glasses, or ramekins if you prefer.

Allow the possets to set in the fridge for at least 3 hours, or overnight. Before serving, sprinkle a light top layer of cantuccini crumbs on to the possets and finish off with a few strands of lemon zest. Serve with a biscuit each.

Fig leaf crème brûlée

If I see crème brûlée on a restaurant menu, I find it hard not to order it. Once you've practised this recipe a few times, you can knock it up in a matter of minutes for almost as many people as you need (twenty? no problem!). For my crème brûlée inspiration I need to mention two people. First off, Alastair Little, a wonderful chef, sadly no longer with us, whose restaurant in Notting Hill I ate at many times. I used the crème brûlée recipe in his book *Keep it Simple* so many times that the page eventually fell out … but by then I no longer needed the recipe. The second person to thank is Margot Henderson, another brilliant chef, who was my recent inspiration for the surprising but tasty fig leaf. Its flavour is more figgy than a fig; it tastes just like the aromatic leaf smells. Margot uses it to make ice cream (also delicious).

Feeds 6

Preparation time: 10 minutes, plus at least 2 hours setting

Cooking time: 10–15 minutes

500ml (18fl oz) double cream

1–2 fig leaves, washed

6 egg yolks (see tip)

100g (3½oz) caster sugar

50g (1¾oz) Demerara sugar

Pour the cream into a saucepan, add the fig leaves and warm over a medium heat. You need to bring the cream to scalding point – the moment just before it boils – so keep a careful eye on the pan and stir occasionally. It should take 3–5 minutes.

Meanwhile, put the egg yolks and caster sugar in a large bowl and whisk using a stand mixer or electric beaters on high speed for 1–2 minutes, until thick, pale and creamy.

Remove your now-hot cream from the stove, discard the fig leaves and stir the mix slowly into the egg yolks. Give your saucepan a quick rinse and put all the crème brûlée mix back into the pan. Return it to a medium heat.

This is the crucial bit of cooking: you need to stir the pan constantly, making sure that your mixture doesn't turn to scrambled egg (which it will do if it gets too hot and/or you don't stir the mixture). Your aim is to get the mixture hot enough to form a custard, but not too hot, or it will split. The mixture will slowly thicken and is ready once it is coating the back of a wooden spoon. Hold your nerve, as it needs to thicken.

Now quickly decant the mixture into a large wide-necked jug through a sieve, then pour the mix from the jug into 6 ramekins. Refrigerate for at least 2 hours, to cool and set.

Up to 2 hours before serving, sprinkle the tops of your now-set crème brûlées with the Demerara sugar, then burn the sugar with a kitchen blowtorch, or under a hot grill, until it melts and forms a crust over the cream (watch it constantly). Cool a little before serving.

Charlie's tip The leftover egg whites will keep, covered, in the fridge for several days and be perfect for my Hazelnut Meringues with Chestnut Cream (see page 228).

Chocolate torte with caramelised hazelnuts

A rich indulgent chocolate pud is often the best thing to round off a proper meal. For me, the secret is to use very good dark chocolate (I have a special penchant for Willie's Cacao). Adding a few nuts into the mix makes the end result all the better. Any chocolate pudding can only be improved when accompanied by whipped cream or crème fraîche. This torte has been perfected over the years by my son Caspar, and is a regular feature in our house.

Feeds 8–10

Preparation time: 10 minutes, plus cooling and chilling

Cooking time: 30–40 minutes

300g (10½oz) butter, cubed: salted or unsalted, whatever is to hand

200g (7oz) dark chocolate (70 per cent cocoa solids works best), broken into pieces

150g (5½oz) granulated sugar

100g (3½oz) blanched hazelnuts, roughly chopped

6 eggs

250ml (9fl oz) double cream

To serve

icing sugar

lashings of whipped cream

toasted hazelnuts

Preheat your oven to 180°C/160°C fan (350°F), Gas Mark 4. Line a 23cm (9 inch) springform cake tin with nonstick baking paper.

Put 200g of the butter and all the chocolate in a heatproof bowl and place it over a small saucepan of simmering water, making sure the bowl does not touch the water. Allow it to melt, then stir.

Put 50g (1¾oz) of the granulated sugar in a medium heavy-based saucepan with 2 tablespoons of water. Heat gently until the sugar dissolves, without stirring, then increase the heat and boil until the sugar turns into a brown caramel: aim for a good colour, but don't let it go too far. Take off the heat and immediately stir in the remaining butter (the mixture will be very hot at this stage). Stir in the nuts over a low heat and cook, stirring, for a couple of minutes, then remove from the heat.

In a large mixing bowl, or ideally a stand mixer, whisk the eggs with the remaining sugar until thick and pale, then stir in the cream. Add the chocolate and butter mixture and the nut caramel to the bowl and use a large metal spoon to fold everything together well, trying to keep the texture as light as possible.

Put the mixture into the prepared tin, place it on a baking sheet and cook in the oven for 30 minutes, or until slightly risen and still a little bit wobbly in the middle (if using a smaller and deeper tin, the torte will take a bit longer, more like 40 minutes).

Allow to cool for 30 minutes or so, then transfer to a fridge to cool all the way through.

Remove from the baking tin and serve cold with a sprinkling of sifted icing sugar over the top and lashings of whipped cream on the side, sprinkled with toasted hazelnuts.

Charlie's tip Best made the day before you are going to eat it and refrigerated overnight, or for rapid cooling I usually put it in the freezer for 1–2 hours.

Pedro Ximenez & date ice cream

Every now and again you are at someone's house having supper … and something appears on the table you haven't had before. And you think: wow! On such occasions, you have to sneak up to your host afterwards and ask if they wouldn't mind terribly sharing that recipe. In this instance, the magic recipe was ice cream, made by my brother Jamie using his small ice-cream maker. I then discovered that it's also easy to make without an ice-cream maker. Pedro Ximenez sherry is a special drink: dark, intense, raisiny and sweet. It's not only the secret ingredient for this ice cream, but a nicely chilled glassful is the perfect accompaniment to the ice cream.

Feeds 4

Preparation time: 30 minutes, plus cooling and chilling

Cooking time: 15 minutes

150g (5½oz) pitted Medjool dates, chopped into small pieces

150ml (¼ pint) Pedro Ximenez sherry

1 vanilla pod

300ml (½ pint) full-fat milk

5 egg yolks

150g (5½oz) caster sugar

375ml (13fl oz) double cream

shortbread, tuile, cantuccini, or other biscuits, to serve

Soak the dates in a small bowl with the sherry for 3–4 hours.

Cut the vanilla pod in half lengthways and scrape out the seeds. Put the seeds and pod into a medium saucepan and pour in the milk. Bring to the boil, then remove immediately from the heat and leave to infuse for 30 minutes.

Put the egg yolks and sugar in a large mixing bowl and whisk with electric beaters for 2–3 minutes, or until pale and mousse-like. Return the milk back to the boil, then strain on to the yolks through a sieve, whisking all the time.

Give the pan a quick rinse and return the mixture to it. Cook over a low heat until the custard is thick enough to just coat the back of a wooden spoon, stirring constantly. Be careful not to let it boil. Remove from the heat, pour into a large heatproof bowl and set aside to cool for 5 minutes. Stir in the cream, then cover and chill for about 1 hour.

Pour the chilled custard mix into a shallow freezerproof container with a lid and freeze until the edges are frozen (1–2 hours). Use a fork or spatula to break up the ice cream thoroughly and mix well. Repeat this process once or twice more, until the mix is very smooth, mixing well after every 40–60 minutes. (You can also make the ice cream using an ice-cream maker.)

Strain the softened dates through a sieve, reserving the liquid. Break up and beat the ice cream for a final time, then stir in the soaked dates and freeze until solid. (If you aren't serving the ice cream the day it is made, keep the soaking liquid in a covered jar in the fridge.)

When ready to serve, leave the ice cream at room temperature for 10–15 minutes to soften before scooping. Divide between small dishes and spoon the reserved date-infused sherry over the top. Serve with biscuits – and ideally a glass of PX!

Hazelnut meringues with chestnut cream

Here's a homage to my lovely wife Claire: she is a brilliant maker of meringues and two of her favourite foods are hazelnuts and chestnuts. Claire mastered her skills as a meringue maker under the instruction of Sholto, a ten-year-old friend of our youngest son. He was round for a 'play date' a good few years ago when Claire was making meringues and bemoaning their inconsistency on rising reliably. She was put straight on her method by Sholto, who told her that it's key to add the sugar one teaspoon at a time. He was right! Delicious with berries or sliced peaches, or with a spiced apple or pear compote.

Feeds 8 / Makes 16 decent-sized meringues

Preparation time: 10 minutes

Cooking time: at least 2 hours

75g (2¾oz) blanched hazelnuts

6 large eggs

300g (10½oz) caster sugar

For the filling

300ml (½ pint) double cream

100g (3½oz) sweet chestnut purée

1 heaped teaspoon caster sugar

Toast the hazelnuts in a small frying pan until lightly browned. Tip on to a work surface, leave to cool for a few minutes, then roughly chop or break into small pieces (a rolling pin will do the trick). They do tend to roll away as you chop or bash, so simply gather up every now and then (or bash in a clean tea towel).

Line 2 large baking trays with nonstick baking paper or reusable baking liners. Preheat the oven to 120°C/100°C fan (250°F), Gas Mark ½.

Separate the eggs, putting the yolks aside for another recipe (try my Fig Leaf Crème Brûlée, see page 222). Whisk the egg whites, in a large mixing bowl with electric beaters, or in a stand mixer, until stiff but not dry, then add 1 teaspoon of the sugar at a time, whisking well between each addition. You want the meringue to form stiff, shiny peaks. Gently fold in three-quarters of the hazelnuts with a large metal spoon.

Using a large soup spoon, put generous, equal-sized blobs of meringue on to the prepared trays, leaving plenty of space between each. Sprinkle with the rest of the hazelnuts. Put the meringues into the oven for 2 hours, or a lower temperature for longer.

When the meringues are cooked, take them out of the oven, allow to cool, then carefully remove from the baking paper. If you are not eating them straight away, they will keep well for at least a couple of weeks in an airtight container.

To serve, put the cream, chestnut purée and sugar in a bowl or stand mixer and whip to soft peaks. Squish a generous dollop of cream between 2 meringue halves.

Frozen berries with a white chocolate sauce

This is one of those recipes that is so simple I had to include it. Made famous by my friend Mark Hix when he was at The Ivy, it's been replicated by many restaurants since and is a great one to have up your sleeve. I think the secret is to be discerning about the berries you use. Rather than buy a bag of mixed frozen berries (which are likely to be of very different sizes), I recommend buying fresh berries and freezing them yourself.

Feeds 6

Preparation time: 5 minutes, plus at least 2 hours freezing

Cooking time: 5 minutes

600g (1lb 5oz) fresh berries, such as a mixture of redcurrants, blueberries, raspberries and blackcurrants

300ml (½ pint) double cream

300g (10½oz) white chocolate (I recommend Green & Black's), broken into small pieces

Pick through your berries and set aside any that are not up to scratch, or are too big. Spread your selected berries on to a large baking tray so they are all nicely separated, then put into the freezer for at least 2 hours.

Make the sauce 5 minutes before you want to eat. Put the cream and white chocolate pieces into a small saucepan, or into a heatproof bowl over a pan of simmering water, if you prefer (make sure the bowl does not touch the water). Cook over a very low heat, stirring occasionally, until the chocolate is melted.

Quickly arrange the frozen berries on some large, flat plates. You want a good mix of berries on each plate.

Pour a generous quantity of the hot white chocolate sauce over each plate of berries and eat immediately.

Charlie's tip You can freeze the berries in advance, tip them into a container and keep them until you want to make this pudding.

Cheese with membrillo

Cheese is the food of the gods and I have to admit to being just a little greedy when it's put in front of me. I'm going to restrict myself to mentioning just four of my favourites – no easy task – and share my recipe for membrillo, their perfect companion. We have a quince tree in our garden and my October ritual is to make a great vat of membrillo, which then appears on every cheeseboard for the rest of the year.

First up on my Cheese Hero list is Banon, a soft cheese from Provence made from goats' milk and wrapped in chestnut or vine leaves. Once started, it's almost impossible to stop eating until it's all gone! Next, Milleens from County Cork in Ireland, a washed cow's milk cheese with the proud heritage of being one of the first cheeses to appear when the Irish and UK farmhouse cheese scene really took off in the 1970s and 1980s. Then to Italy, to celebrate the wonderful Gorgonzola. This famous blue cheese has been made for more than a thousand years in the town of the same name. And finally, Comté, a lovely Alpine classic made by 160 small producers, all adhering to strict standards. You find interesting variations between their cheeses, as well as the bigger difference between winter and summer Comté.

Makes about 2kg (4lb 8oz) membrillo

Preparation time: 10 minutes, plus overnight setting

Cooking time: 2–3 hours, but worth it!

2kg (4lb 8oz) ripe quinces (about 8)

3 lemons, halved

granulated sugar: equal weight to purée (about 1.5–1.7kg / 3lb 5oz–3lb 10oz)

Wash the quinces and cut them roughly into large chunks (no need to peel or core). Put in a large saucepan, or jam pan, with the lemons and barely cover with cold water. Bring to the boil and simmer until the fruit has all become soft (30–40 minutes).

Strain off most of the liquid, keeping back about 100ml (3½fl oz), and discard the lemon halves. Put your cooked quince through a mouli-légumes, or a sieve (use a spoon or ladle to press down on it), to remove the core, pips and skin, leaving you with a quince purée.

Weigh your purée, then weigh out an equal amount of sugar. Put both in your cleaned-out pan and cook over a very low heat for 1 hour or more, stirring occasionally, and, towards the end, almost constantly, so it does not burn. The membrillo is ready when it has turned deep maroon in colour and has thickened to the point that – when you pull your wooden spoon through it – the base of the pan shows for a few seconds. Watch out for spluttering paste, as the mixture is very hot.

Pour your hot membrillo mix into a shallow dish lined with nonstick baking paper and allow to cool and set at least overnight; you want to be able to cut it easily into pieces.

Once set, I cut the membrillo cake into squares, each about 16cm (4 inches), wrap each in baking paper, tie with kitchen string and store in my fridge, or in airtight boxes in a cool place, until needed. It will last a year or more. Serve the membrillo with your wonderful cheeseboard of delectable cheeses, crackers and fruit.

Index

First published in Great Britain in
2024 by Mitchell Beazley, an imprint
of Octopus Publishing Group Ltd
Carmelite House
50 Victoria Embankment
London EC4Y 0DZ
www.octopusbooks.co.uk

An Hachette UK Company
www.hachette.co.uk

Text copyright © Charlie Bigham 2024
Photography and illustrations
copyright © Bigham's Limited 2024

ISBN 978 1 78472 949 3

A CIP catalogue record for this book is
available from the British Library.

Printed and bound in Italy.

10 9 8 7 6 5 4 3 2 1

Photographer: David Loftus
Illustrator: Emily Sutton
Book Designer: Lawrence Morton
Contributing Editor: Hattie Ellis
Recipe Tester: Justine Patterson
Food Stylist: Jodene Jordan
Props Stylist: Claire Bigham

Publisher: Alison Starling
Senior Managing Editor:
  Sybella Stephens
Copy Editor: Lucy Bannell
Creative Director: Jonathan Christie
Senior Production Manager:
  Katherine Hockley